Science and Religion in the
Thought of Nicolas Malebranche

SCIENCE
AND RELIGION
IN THE THOUGHT OF
Nicolas
Malebranche

BY MICHAEL E. HOBART

THE UNIVERSITY OF

NORTH CAROLINA PRESS

CHAPEL HILL

B1897
H63
1982

Library of Congress Cataloging in Publication Data

Hobart, Michael E., 1944–
Science and religion in the thought of Nicolas
Malebranche.

Bibliography: p.
Includes index.
1. Malebranche, Nicolas, 1638–1715. I. Title.
B1897.H63   194   81-7419
ISBN 0-8078-1487-3   AACR2

For Marcia

Contents

Contents

Acknowledgments

Although most of the intellectual debts incurred in the creation of this book are acknowledged in the notes, there are a number of colleagues, acquaintances, and friends whose tireless or timely contributions deserve special recognition. I am particularly grateful to the Committee on the First Books Program, sponsored by the American Historical Association in cooperation with the Association of American University Presses, and to its chairman, Professor Felix Gilbert. Besides the committee's endorsement of the manuscript for publication, readers for the committee provided a careful and helpful editorial appraisal. Others who read the manuscript, or significant portions of it, and offered salutary critical suggestions include Professors John P. Losee, Burleigh T. Wilkins, Dominick A. Iorio, W. Jay Reedy, Richard Lebrun, and Alan D. Beyerchen. Hilda Cooper prepared the manuscript in various stages, combining with her invaluable secretarial talents a fund of patience that, try as I might, I could never exhaust.

I am deeply indebted to three individuals who have had an extensive involvement with the book in a broader capacity. Leonard Marsak of the University of California, Santa Barbara, has supported the project from its earliest appearance through the final revisions, reading drafts and furnishing the mentorial guidance and encouragement a young scholar needs. Robert Cruden of Lewis and Clark College—teacher, colleague, friend—has been a constant point of reference for me, proving by example, as well as by exhortation, that sanity and scholarship, hard work and honesty are not all mutually exclusive in the history profession. Mark Gabbert of the University of Manitoba has given me and my work incalculable sustenance. In a world without end where words and ideas are the staff of life, our many long discussions, frequently ending only with dawn or exhaustion (whichever has come first), have been a continual source of learning, enrichment, and delight.

Without the support and assistance of all these people the task of conceiving, researching, writing, and preparing the manuscript would have been far more painful, perhaps impossible. Writing is a stubborn process; that I was too stubborn to pay them more heed is no doubt the source of the errors that remain.

Finally, I must acknowledge with both pride and humility the influence of my wife, Marcia; though not footnoted, her presence is discernible throughout the book. She has participated in its every phase, experiencing with me its intellectual excitements and frustrations, sharing the sacrifices it has exacted, and putting up with the practical demands and disruptions it has brought home. More to the point, she teaches me daily that 'being' is not an abstract category but a concrete, living reality. This book is for her—very small payment for such a very large lesson.

Science and Religion in the
Thought of Nicolas Malebranche

CHAPTER I

Introduction:
The Models of 'Substance'
and 'Number'

Few theoretical problems have commanded as much intellectual energy as articulating the relation between what we know and what we believe, between science and religion. Beginning with man's earliest and most tentative attempts at using his mind to comprehend the mysteries of his experience, the history of this relation extends unbroken to our own day. In the seventeenth century the scientific revolution initiated a new chapter in the chronicle of these efforts, particularly during the last quarter of the century as the conventions of a scientific "method" gained wider acceptance and agreement among the intellectual public.[1] At that time assimilating new canons of epistemology into an inherited body of theological and religious discourse loomed as a primary concern of many literati, natural philosophers, and theologians. In France, Nicolas Malebranche flourished at the hub of this activity. His lifelong vocation as a member of the Oratory united a commitment to theological studies of his Christian faith with an interest in contemporary science, especially the accomplishments of his predecessor, René Descartes. Moreover, he explicitly desired to consummate "modern," Cartesian science—just as he believed Thomas Aquinas had perfected the science of Aristotle and antiquity—by integrating it thoroughly into a religious view of the world consistent with Catholicism.

These labors brought Malebranche into immediate, if often ambiguous, contact with major contemporary intellectual currents. From a milieu saturated with Augustinianism, neo-Platonism (Malebranche is sometimes referred to as the "French Plato"), Cartesian rationalism, empiricism, scepticism, libertinism, and scholasticism, it is scarcely surprising that tensions emerged in his thought and that Malebranche seemed at times unsure of how to formulate and resolve issues germane to his central vocation. Indeed, of seventeenth-century intellectuals none has been more perplexing than Malebranche, both to his contemporaries and to subsequent generations of scholars. This perplexity has been captured inimitably by Paul Hazard: "He had at least some of the virtues that go to the making of a saint. Open-hearted and utterly guileless as he was, he was subtle, too, and stubbornly determined. Nothing in the world would have induced him to abandon his ideas; when they provoked difficulties, he had a way, peculiarly his own, of plunging into still more difficulties, till at length the tangle became inextricable; then he was elated."[2] Malebranche's elation, not ours; we are left with the tangle. Are ideas independent beings or modifications of mind? Are there two types of extension or one? Do numbers refer to existents or to relations about existents? Do the truths of magnitude supersede those of perfection, or is the opposite reading in order? Is there one infinity, or are there several infinities? Does reason prove God's existence, or is God necessary as the guarantor of reason (the "Cartesian circle")? Are science, mathematics, and epis-

4

temology logically prior to religion, faith, and metaphysics, or vice versa? These and many similar questions attend even the most cursory acquaintance with Malebranche's writings and permeate his efforts to relate knowledge and belief. Malebranche is seldom overtly helpful in resolving such questions. His readers frequently have struggled to capture one or more of his abstruse opinions, only to have him apparently change his meaning in a subsequent passage—occasioning further questions and frustrations, not to mention oaths, from his audience.

More so than with other thinkers, then, the burden of understanding Malebranche weighs heavily on the reader. One needs some sort of guidance to relate what Martial Gueroult calls Malebranche's "immense philosophical cathedral"[3]—his soaring and complex philosophical visions—to the building blocks of his intellectual architecture. One strategy that has yielded increasingly significant results in intellectual history is the seeking of "deep structures"[4] in an intellectual's discourse, the looking beneath the surface level of exposition to elicit the structure of the imagination that gave the exposition its force, direction, and substance. This method of analysis appears all the more attractive in the case of Malebranche. Scholars who have failed to penetrate the surface of his writings frequently tend to infer from his contradictory statements that he was a philosophical weakling scarcely worth a second look,[5] or they meticulously and laboriously wend their way through the gossamers of French logic and metaphysics to find a harmony that is as tangled as the Oratorian himself.[6] Searching out the structures behind Malebranche's visions carries the hope of untangling the web and of doing so in a manner that clarifies rather than obscures his thought.

To implement this strategy, two intellectual models will guide the present analysis. Creation and use of these models is based largely on the theoretical justification provided in Max Black's superlative essay, "Models and Archetypes."[7] Black develops the notion that a model constitutes a "sustained and systematic metaphor" that has the capacity to suggest new inferences, novel hypotheses, and speculations. A model, he contends, is not an "ornamental substitute" for pure thinking, historical or scientific, but a distinctive mode of achieving insight through the union of two domains of discourse, primary and secondary. The primary domain comprises the original field of investigation in which some "facts" and "regularities" have been established (the writings of Malebranche in the present instance) but in which a need for further mastery is felt. The secondary domain, that of the model, describes some entities—objects, materials, mechanisms, systems, or structures—as belonging to a relatively "unproblematic, more familiar, or better-organized" sphere. Inferences and assumptions that can be formulated within the secondary domain are then correlated with and "independently checked against known or predicted data in the primary domain." The key to understanding the entire transaction is the "identity of structure," which in favorable cases permits the assertions made about the secondary domain "to yield insight into the original field of interest." A good model then requires that we have an "intuitive grasp ('Gestalt knowledge')" of its capacities so that we can "freely *draw inferences*" from it. If we cannot, then the model is sterile and closes off investigation, rather than providing us assistance.

Black elaborates this theory in a description of four types of models—scale, analogue, theoretical, and submerged—each of which possesses notable features for the intellectual historian. Like the scale model, the intellectual models used here are *of* something; they have referents. The referents may be variously described as visions, intuitions, or imaginations—the "deep structures"—that underlay Malebranche's written expression. The essential feature of the analogue model is the reproduction of the structure of the primary domain—in this case the structure of Malebranche's imagination—in a different medium or different sphere of discourse, one more familiar. Such a structural reproduction, further, is more than a "heuristic fiction" that typifies analogues and that provides only an "isomorphic" identity with the original domain; like the theoretical model it has "existential content." The models used here, in other words, are not mere hypotheses about the coherence of Malebranche's thought but existential statements that purport to explain it and the problems therein. This claim is made because of the "analogical extension" that is essential to the fourth type of model Black describes, the "submerged model," otherwise termed the "conceptual archetype" or simply "archetype." The archetype refers to the systematic repertoire of ideas that a thinker relies on when he describes some domain to which those ideas do not immediately and literally apply. One example here will be Malebranche's implicit use of mathematical expressions, such as the ideas of infinity and relation, to refer to God. The archetype, which Black notes is roughly synonymous with a variety of terms (more common to intellectual history)—"root metaphor," "ultimate frame of reference," "ultimate presupposition," "world hypothesis," or dominating "system of concepts"—thus serves to transform inchoate areas of investigation and imagination into cognition, to transform intuition into expression. Although these dominant metaphors will always be at least partially submerged in an intellectual's expression, they can be recognized by another observer and brought to conscious attention. This is a function of the intellectual historian. Using intellectual models then will provide us with the conceptual tools for pursuing our strategy, for achieving insight into Malebranche's writings, for making explicit his implicit or submerged intellectual structures, and for perceiving connections in his thought hitherto left undetected.

What sorts of connections are we seeking? In short, those

inferences and assumptions that were altered during the seventeenth century under the impact of a new epistemology. The scientific revolution, Herbert Butterfield tells us, "outshines everything since the rise of Christianity" because it "changed the character of men's habitual mental operations."[8] We are equally assured by many historians that the key to the new mental operations was mathematics. In one of the many perceptive comments that were a mark of his genius, Ernst Cassirer stated that, before the Renaissance, mathematics had been considered an element of thought but that afterward, from Leonardo and Galileo on, it gradually assumed the position of a central "force" in Western intellectual life.[9] Descartes himself is usually considered by scholars as the first major intellectual figure in modern times to be sensitive to the influence of mathematics on traditional philosophical concerns. It is the specific nature of this central force and its implications for traditional thought that need further investigation in Malebranche. This involves more than an adjectival characterization of mathematical thought—often described as "certain, precise, and exact,"[10] and employing univocal deduction, first principles, and a host of like methods. It means isolating specifically the essential inferences and assumptions of mathematics and indicating how these became incorporated as constituents of thought in a broader context. Once this is done the dilemmas, tensions, and conflicts so readily apparent at the surface of Malebranche's writings may be understood in relation to the deeper, structural transformation of intellectual life that accompanied the scientific revolution.

For Malebranche's thought was mired in an historical struggle. On the one hand, traditional intellectual patterns and assumptions, herein noted by the model of 'substance', maintained much of their power and attraction. On the other hand, newly emerging patterns and assumptions, keyed on mathematics and the model of 'number', were equally alluring. It is within the framework of this struggle that his conjunction of science and religion must be sought. The remaining task of this chapter, accordingly, will be to delineate the elements of the models of 'substance' and 'number' that will serve as the guides for the ensuing discussion.[11]

The structure of thought inherited from Aristotle, aptly dubbed the "traditional way of thinking" by Ortega y Gasset,[12] was primarily classificatory in nature, dividing the bits and pieces of reality into their general and specific characteristics, sorting them into collections according to what appeared as common elements among the pieces.[13] The creation of these collections presupposed only the inexhaustible multiplicity of things and the ability of the mind to select elements common to some of them.[14] Facing this sensate and undifferentiated multiplicity, the mind absorbed through the senses an image that it then transformed into a "mental extract" by fixing its attention on one aspect within the field of imagery. This "mental extract" served to differentiate the specific properties included within it from the remaining sensa, thus determining its limits as a concept or term.[15] Terms provided in turn the tools for logical ordering and classifying. (The Greeks called "mental extracts" the *logos*, and hence what was said about the web of extracts constituted logical theory.[16]) Those terms possessing similar properties were grouped into subspecies; subspecies were grouped by common features into species; species were classed into genera, and so on. As each grouping was formed, the species became the logical modification of the genera under which it was subsumed; it added those characteristics that gave the genera specific content. Conversely, each genus was an abstraction above the species that were contained within it and provided the species with their general properties or form. Strictly speaking, species, all particular cognitions, could not be deduced from genera but were differentiated within the framework of generic structures. The result was the emergence of a firm, pyramidal order and division of reality, an ideal hierarchy of genera and species.

But an inherent difficulty riddled this conception. By extending the generic concept it became increasingly void of content, until at the highest levels the most general concepts no longer possessed any specific content.[17] At this point their meaning and value as cognitive terms were obviated by their position of transcendence over the entire logical hierarchy. Thus the concept 'being' in its broadest usage contained everything, and at the same time nothing, for from 'being' one could infer only 'non-being' not any knowledge per se. Ortega noted this epistemic difficulty and labeled the traditional concept of 'being' a monstrosity: "Ens [sic] in terms of the pure 'general' and the pure 'abstract' is neither a genus nor has it species. It is said—positively or negatively—of everything, and this makes it apparently into a thing so empty that it provides no 'matter' capable of being established as a species."[18] It would appear that the greater one's knowledge, the closer one ventured toward the meaningless. As Cassirer observed, even though the intention behind the process of producing generic terms was positive—insofar as the higher and more general concepts were meant to be the logical grounding of the lower, constituting the lower's essential form and making it intelligible— each mental act of differentiation excluded far more than it included, rendering the entire process negative and arbitrary:

> The traditional rule . . . for the formation of the generic concept contains in itself no guarantee that this end [the establishment of a valid generic concept] will be actually achieved. In fact, there is nothing to assure us that the common properties, which we select from any arbitrary collection of objects, include the truly typical features, which characterize and determine the total structures of

the members of the collection. We may borrow a drastic example from Lotze: If we group cherries and meat together under the attributes red, juicy, and edible, we do not thereby attain a valid logical concept, but a meaningless combination of words.[19]

To eliminate this fortuity, Aristotle had been compelled to rely upon a feature beyond the logical process itself, one that in fact underscored the process. It was his metaphysics and, in particular, the idea of substance to which his logical theories had constant reference. Aristotle's definition of substance left little doubt as to the primacy of metaphysics over logic and epistemology. Substance had two senses: first, the "ultimate substratum," which is not predicated of anything and on which all else is predicated; secondly, that which is a "this" and which can be differentiated from all else.[20] By assuming as real a world composed of substrata and differentia, the mental acts of grouping and comparing things became the method by which to discover the essential structure of that reality.[21] Again Cassirer: "The determination of the concept according to its next higher genus and its specific difference reproduces the process by which the real substance successively unfolds itself in its special forms of being."[22] In other words, terms, that is, subjects and modifications (or predicates), and the logical relations of genus and species between terms derived their meaning from a reality structured of substances and their attributes, the essences of which were both reflected and captured by those terms. Knowing for Aristotle, in short, meant to answer the question: "What is it to be a certain kind of thing?"[23] From which it followed that properties such as quantity, space and time determinations, and in general any nongeneric relations did not exist in and for themselves but merely as dependent and subordinate features of being. They added only supplementary and external modifications (accidents) to the real nature of substance. This nature or being, in both its generality and its specificity, was a prior and determining condition for all knowledge.[24]

A complete epistemology and metaphysics thus revolved about this central idea of substance, the assumption of being—the parts of which were structured into a generic hierarchy—that stood at the core of ancient and medieval thought. For this reason we may say that the "traditional way of thinking" was founded upon the model of 'substance', since this idea in its many ramifications provided the paradigm, implicit and explicit, for much of the intellectual matrix of nearly two millenia.[25] Reference to this model signifies the tendency to form abstractions that follow the patterns and processes of classifying described above and carry the assumption of an ontological priority: thought reflecting upon being, which in turn determines the paths thought will travel.

Much evidence suggests that this model of 'substance' still held powerful sway over the mental habits of the early seventeenth century, although cracks in its structure were beginning to appear. Criticism came from several sources. The scientific achievements of Copernicus, Kepler, Galileo, and others progressively undermined Aristotelian physics and cosmology. Intellectual debates during the Reformation raised the question of the "criteria" for knowledge of religious truths, while the "*crise pyrrhonienne*," represented most lucidly by Montaigne, mounted a general attack on all knowledge.[26] Moreover, a new spirit of critical empiricism, punctuated by the aphorisms and observations of Francis Bacon, was gaining credence. Bacon is usually and rightly seen as the most forward-looking of his contemporaries in his attitude toward empirical observations, for while traditional thought was empirical, or "sensist" to use Ortega's term, it did not countenance a critical and experimental posture in the use of the senses to wrest secrets from nature.[27] But even as Bacon looked ahead he did not escape the pervasiveness of traditional mental habits; the form of his science was firmly grounded in 'substance': "For all nature rises to a point like a pyramid. Individuals, which lie at the base of nature, are infinite in number; these are collected into Species, which are themselves manifold; the Species rise again into Genera; which also by continual gradations are contracted into more universal generalities, so that at last nature seems to end as it were in unity."[28] No paragon of modern thinking here. Nonetheless, as the attacks on traditional thought increased, both in degree and kind, reflective minds were compelled to seek alternative ways of thinking, and of these the most satisfying came to be that founded upon mathematics and the model of 'number'.

The concept of number as we know it did not achieve explicit formulation until the late nineteenth and early twentieth centuries. In this period investigations resulting in the "arithmetization of mathematics" demonstrated that, in order to understand mathematics in theory, one needed to grasp the principles of mathematical operations in their most elementary expression—arithmetic, the fundamentals of which presupposed and rested upon the idea of number. As an introduction to the idea of number and the model of mathematical thinking it suggests for an analysis of Cartesianism, we may look with profit to the results of these investigations as they apply to two questions: What is the nature of the mathematical mind? What are the features of the number concept itself? In an admirably clear essay entitled "Intuition and Logic in Mathematics," the noted French mathematician, Henri Poincaré, addressed himself to the first of these questions.[29] Poincaré distinguished between two types of mathematicians: the "analysts," who are preoccupied with logic and proceed step by trenchant step; and the "geometers," who are guided by intuition and often make "quick but sometimes precarious conquests." What separates the two is not simply a manner of dealing with mathematical problems but the nature of their minds, which cannot be laid aside whenever a new subject is approached. The analytical mind reduces everything to a consideration of series and their analytical transformations—analysis treated as a "prolongation of arithmetic"—while the intuitionist confronts the world without, allowing images or pictures—"seeing in space" —to dominate his thought. The latter tires quickly of long calculations; the former has little patience with the "subjectivism" of intuitions. Both, Poincaré argued, have been and are indispensable for progress in mathematics. Logic, when pushed to its limits, results in tautology; nothing new is discovered. Intuition without analytical foundations may give nice "pictures" but not the certainty of an analytically rigorous and formal proof of its claims.

Not only are both mentalities indispensible for the development of mathematics, Poincaré continued, in rare exceptions both will be fused into one truly creative mind, a man of genius who can discover new truths and also demonstrate with complete logical rigor their validity, a man who is at once an analyst and a geometer. But how does this mind work, since the analyst, by definition, refuses to allow intuitive imagination into his mental operations, while the geometer lacks the analyst's rigor? In answering this Poincaré observed that there are many kinds of intuition, including direct appeals to the senses and imagination as well as generalization through induction. But only a special intuition, that of "pure number," is able to "create the real mathematical reasoning." By means of the intuition of "pure number," mathematicians have, without the aid of senses and imagination, a "direct sense of what constitutes the unity of a piece of reasoning." Their intuition is of a "principle of internal unity"—that is, of "pure logical forms." The intuition of number is thus a "higher" mode of intuition that synthesizes logic, the instrument of demonstration that alone can give certainty, and the "lower" forms of intuition that are the instruments of invention.[30]

How striking is the thought of Descartes compared with this description of the mathematical mind! Descartes' own mathematical efforts were directed toward the synthetic end of combining analysis and geometry, in addition to which his expressed desire was to develop method and epistemology with the dual goals of discovering new truths and demonstrating their validity with logical certainty. He often criticized the methods and aims of scholastic logic for being mere explications of what one already knows, providing no addition to man's knowledge.[31] At the same time new knowledge was insufficient if it lacked a logical foundation based on complete analytic demonstration, which he sought to provide throughout his works.[32] But beyond these considerations it was Descartes' passion for an internal unity of all thought that calls to mind Poincaré's notion of mathematical intuition, for the image of unity that Descartes struck upon was radically different from that perceived by scholastic thinkers and bore close affinity to the intuition of number.

If the mathematical mind, then, such as that of Descartes, intuits number as its guiding activity, the concept of number and the implications it entails provide the form and direction that intuition takes. Tobias Dantzig, in a penetrating and approachable study of the number concept, summarized this idea by noting that all mathematical processes rest on "Number and Function; that Function itself can in the ultimate be reduced to Number; that the general concept of Number rests in turn on the properties we ascribe to the natural sequence: one, two, three. . . ."[33] Further, a most significant feature of the "natural sequence" is that its members are not things, nor objects in an ideal sense, but consist solely of relations between things or objects.[34] These relations differ vastly from those that classify things according to their genus and species, although the latter type of grouping does exist in an accidental sense in the number realm.[35] Number relations are founded upon two principles: the principle of correspondence and the principle of recurrence. Together these two principles define the number concept in both its cardinal and its ordinal aspects.[36]

The principle of correspondence is the heart of the cardinal concept of number. It states that there is a correlation between the members of any two collections: for each member of a collection *a* there is one, and only one, member of collection *b* to which it corresponds and vice-versa. An auditorium, for example, has an assemblage of seats; a crowd of people enters and claims them, each person claiming one seat only. If the two collections correspond exactly with neither empty seats nor standing people, then they are said to have the same cardinal number. Whereas this example refers to groups of real objects, in the history of mathematics there has been a growth from correspondence between real collections to a correspondence between real and model collections—such as the English tally stick or pebbles (the Latin term for pebble is *calculus*)—and finally to a correspondence between real collections and ideal models, the latter utilizing the number word and the number symbol.[37] Only with the introduction of model collections does number per se truly begin to emerge, for models, and especially ideal models, involve an abstract element in that their members can stand for or signify any other objects. This correspondence pervades all mathematics. Thus applied mathematics involves correspondence between real and ideal collections; Newton's formula for gravity, $F=ma$, holds true because of the correlation between number symbols and units of force, mass, and distance perceived or assumed in nature. Pure mathematics, on the other hand, employs exclusively ideal models. In the equation $a=bc$, members of classes *b* and *c* that are combined according to the designated operation—in this case multiplication—must correspond exactly to class *a*, in addition to which *a*, *b*, and *c* themselves may correspond to any other classes of number symbols, provided the relation between those symbols remains identical to the relation between *a*, *b*, and *c*. The cardinal concept then is defined to mean the one-to-one correlation between discrete members, or units, of any two or more classes; it involves no counting.[38]

But a counting process is necessary for mathematics and is implied by the cardinal concept itself, for the meaning of any collection of number symbols cannot be arbitrarily restricted to its correlation with any other collection. "The specific meaning of 'four' or 'seven' could never result from the bare placing together of any number of groups of 'four' or 'seven' elements; the individual groups must first be determined as ordered sequences of elements."[39] Stated another way, the members of a collection must be arranged in a "natural" or "ordered" sequence that "progresses in the sense of growing magnitude," and each member must be assigned a term in that "*natural sequence*: one, two, three. . . ."[40] The term assigned to the last member is called the ordinal number of the collection, and assumed in these assignations is a premise critical to the operations of arithmetic: one can always pass from a number to its successor. In short, the process of reasoning recurs indefinitely or more accurately, infinitely. Hence the ordinal concept is called the "principle of recurrence."[41] Moreover, in assuming that each number has a successor, the counting process postulates the continuous realm of numbers, an "arithmetic continuum" that is "everywhere dense," unbroken and unterminated. This means, first, that between any two numbers there can be interpolated an infinity of other numbers and, second, that there is no conceivable end to the process of counting—it may be extrapolated to infinity. Thus the ordinal concept expresses the unity and continuity of number whereas the cardinal concept reveals the discreteness of elements or units that are singled out from the number realm.[42]

From these two general properties of number emerge four further aspects of the number concept that carry particular significance for understanding Cartesianism in the seventeenth century. First, the primary relations based on the principles of correspondence and recurrence are those of 'equal to', 'greater than', and 'less than'. These three relations are necessary in order to ground the associative, commutative, and distributive properties of numbers and also to lay the foundations of arithmetical operations and procedures, including the basic four of addition, subtraction, multiplication, and division. Friedrich Waismann observes that the primary relations, when given rigorous definitions by means of conventional "calculating rules" governing "concept formation," are the basis for a rigorous construction of an arithmetic of integers and, by extension, a theory of rational and real numbers and their operations. Thus, for example, the relation of equality is defined rigorously as reflexive ($a=a$), symmetric (if $a=b$, then $b=a$), and transitive (if $a=b$ and $b=c$, then $a=c$), while the relations greater and smaller are irreflexive (a is never greater or smaller than a), asymmetric (if $a>b$, then b cannot be $>a$; if $a<b$, then b cannot be $<a$), and transitive (if $a>b$ and $b>c$, then $a>c$; if $a<b$ and $b<c$, then $a<c$). These definitions of equal, greater, and smaller, initially formed to describe the relations between integers, extend to the higher classes of numbers, enabling a "mapping" of integers and their arithmetic functions into rationals and rationals into real numbers.[43] Likewise the higher operations such as algebra, which may be seen as a more generalized form of arithmetic, and calculus, which is a generalization of algebraic functions, remain firmly grounded in the primary relations of equal, greater, smaller, as they are derived

from the concept of number in both its cardinal and ordinal senses.[44]

Second, in contrast to the pattern of thinking character-ized by genus and species, abstraction based upon 'number' is more thoroughgoing while remaining 'closer' to the phenomena through one-to-one correspondence, for nowhere is there any necessary ontological connection between the content of a sensory intuition and the rational extract or concept that is drawn from it.[45] Although the cardinal concept bears some similarity to the generic term described above, there is one very significant difference between the two. The "mental ex-tract" of correspondence, which places classes of the same number of members under the same number term, eliminates the sensory content of the term by eliciting pure abstract units —vis-à-vis a sensate quality—from the field of apprehension. For example, the generic concept asserts a classification of perceived characteristics, such as the classifying of men, dogs, and any other beings with a backbone under the heading 'verte-brates', while the cardinal concept claims only that a class of n number of units that corresponds to another class of n number of units is subsumed under the same heading 'n'. There is thus an *act* of perceiving similarity between classes of n units, but the resultant term is totally void of any sensory content. From this it follows that any meaning attending the number realm itself can have, in contemporary terms, no "extrasystemic" references,[46] no necessary relation with anything outside its own structure or serial order. The number realm is a "system of ideal objects whose whole content is exhausted in their mutual relations. The 'essence' of numbers is completely ex-pressed in their positions."[47] The traditional form-content dis-tinction, therefore, makes no sense in mathematics per se because form and content are mutually included in the logical notions of position, series, and relation—in short, number.

Also, universality cannot be simply an increasing generality that is derived generically from essences as with the model of 'substance', but constitutes an ideal realm of relations to which any matter or series of objects is potentially applicable. The actual correspondence of material content with the realm of pure mathematics is, as some men in the seventeenth century came to see, a question of experiment, that is, applied mathematics. Yet experiment, strictly speaking, is irrelevant to the meaning of the purely logical realm of number, the realm to which Poincaré referred when he described the intuition of pure number as the intuition of the complete logical unity of a piece of reasoning.

Third, since number relations, not generic terms and their relations, constitute the number realm, manipulations of relations with the object of establishing new ones make up the operations of mathematics. Every number is itself nothing more than a relation, for example, 2 is simply the ratio of $^2/_1$, and the establishment of relations between numbers achieves not an agreement between terms but between propositions. The form of mathematical statements is thus: "If such a proposition is true of *anything*, then such and such another proposition is true."[48] If $2+4$ is true (of apples, units of force, or whatever), then $5+1$ must be equally true. Again, in a strict sense, it is of no consequence to the meaning of the relation whether or not the first proposition is true *of* anything. This characteristic is extremely important and played a capital, though often implicit, role in the thought of Descartes and Malebranche.

A fourth mark of 'number' derives from the inexhaustibility of the counting process. At first glance infinity might appear to lead to a serious difficulty. To establish a mathematical law, a principle that governs the relations in a series, is to claim that a particular relation holds for any number throughout the series. But since there is an infinity of numbers, such a law could never be fully tested (assuming an "open" series) and therefore never be fully certain. At this point the mathematician's faith joins forces with his logic. Recognizing that mathematical laws are not inductively established, in the sense of empirical induction, and that pure deduction, when reduced to tautology, is insufficient to establish new laws, the mathematician asserts that laws can be and are established on the assumption of recurrence. Whenever a relation is true for any number of a series, n, and is shown to be true as well for its successor, $n+1$, it may be said to hold true for *any* number in the series whatsoever because of the mind's ability to conceive the indefinite repetition of the mental act once the act has been proven possible. Once the relation is demonstrated for n and $n+1$, $n+1$ simply becomes the new n and the proof can be restated ad infinitum. The principle governing the relation is thus established by "mathematical induction." In both its interpolative and extrapolative senses, therefore, the idea of infinity, which is derived neither from experience nor logic per se, is intrinsic to the fabric of mathematics. It is a necessary assumption without which mathematical thinking could not occur. The Pythagoreans discovered this truth, much to their horror, at a very early date.[49]

Summarizing then, the model of 'number' in this work will refer to the tendency to order ideas according to the following criteria: (a) the serial relations of 'equal to', 'greater than', and 'less than', which enable operations to be performed within the natural series of increasing magnitude, the arithmetic continuum; (b) the one-to-one correspondence between ideas and objects or between ideas and other ideas, with the implication that between realms of ideas and objects there can be no extra-systemic references to establish the meaning of any realm; (c) the formulation of relations between propositions in the hypothetical form, 'if . . . then', rather than generic relations between "mental extracts" or terms; (d) and finally, the process of reasoning by recurrence with its accompanying sense of infinity. Other features of the 'number' model will be introduced as required; for the present these need be acknowledged as the most significant. Not that all the above characteristics are crystal clear in Descartes or Malebranche. But just as the history of mathematics reveals that mathematicians have often used ideas and procedures without possessing fully explicit justification and awareness of them, so does Cartesian thought in the seventeenth century, in its two leading exponents, reveal a reliance upon the 'number' model and a concern for the features intrinsic to it. The present task is to show this reliance and concern and their consequences for the relation between science and religion, thereby rendering explicit what is often left unsaid or merely assumed about thought in the seventeenth century—that it begins to reflect not upon being but upon itself.

CHAPTER 2

'Number' and 'Substance' in Descartes

Although the late sixteenth and early seventeenth centuries witnessed widespread intellectual crisis, as Richard Popkin and other scholars have indicated, they were nonetheless a time of growth and innovation in mathematical thought. Revival of Platonism during the Renaissance had combined with the discovery and new translation of ancient works on conic sections, astronomy, trigonometry, and the like to renew and propagate interest in pure mathematics. Too, practical innovations in areas such as navigation, instrument construction, and accounting further encouraged many men to examine the "imagination mathematical." With this interest motivating study, new developments were not long in coming. One of the most singular achievements was that of François Viète (1540–1603), who first suggested and devised general rules for algebraic notation, thereby transforming that science and mathematics with it from, at best, a syncopated algebra into a fully symbolized system of thought.[1] Others, notably Thomas Hariot (1560–1621), furthered this symbolization by devising ways of manipulating and solving equations of higher degrees. Descartes himself established the system of algebraic notation still used today, and far more important he united the new algebra with Euclidean geometry in the creation of coordinate or analytic geometry. Such innovations helped stimulate philosophical reflection on mathematics and especially on its use and manipulation of abstract symbols.

That Descartes began to seriously tap this mine of intellectual wealth lay at the basis of his principal philosophical achievements. His writings yield ample evidence of a desire to extend methods and insights gleaned from mathematics to more general propositions regarding method, science, and epistemology. As the noted Dutch historian of science, E. J. Dijksterhuis, remarked, Descartes "virtually identified mathematics and science," not simply in the sense that mathematics ministers to science, but in the deeper connotation that the mind produces a unified knowledge of nature by its own efforts in the same manner that it produces mathematics.[2] Moreover, many of the tensions found in his work stem from his attempts to articulate these new insights within the framework of traditional philosophy. For present purposes we need to sketch his reliance on 'number' and 'substance' and the conflict between these two submerged models before turning in more detail to Malebranche.

The most prominent manifestation of 'number' in Descartes' discourse is found in his writings on method, beginning with the *Rules for the Direction of the Mind*, which was probably composed about 1628, although not published until 1701, long after his death. Descartes wrote the *Rules* to consolidate his early thoughts on method and epistemology, and they constituted his first major attempt to realize his dream of a unified science.[3] In the opening passages he heralded a new sense of order, one which denied the "incommunicability of the genera"[4] by claiming that the "sciences taken all together are identical with human wisdom, which always remains one and the same, however applied to different subjects."[5] Indeed the "discovery of an order" must be considered the chief purpose of the treatise, since in Descartes' words order was "practically its sole subject."[6] The *Rules* further indicated that the new sense of order would be clearly mathematical, founded upon 'number' and constituted by the relations implied in the number concept. Early in the work, after having stated that method consists in "the order and disposition of the objects towards which our mental vision must be directed,"[7] Descartes postulated that ordering and disposing objects were to be accomplished by separating those that were simple from those that were more complex. To achieve this separation it was necessary to mark the "interval, greater, less, or equal" between the "facts" in any series of cognitions. By so arranging "facts" in a series, one observed their "correlative connection and natural order," thereby obtaining genuine knowledge of the objects. This knowledge stood in sharp contrast to the traditional procedure of locating objects in "some ontological genus, such as the categories employed by Philosophers in their classification." Descartes was so enamored of the new sense of order that he declared it to contain "the chief secret" of his entire method.[8]

The term "facts" in this formulation was employed to signify both simple and complex objects. The former were those "pure and simple essences" grasped by intuition, "the undoubting conception of an unclouded and attentive mind,"[9] while the latter were the objects deduced through a "chain of operations" from the former. Taken in themselves, pure and simple essences were "absolute"; objects deduced from them, though "participating in the same nature," were "relative," and one had to traverse the deductions in order to return to the primary facts that were the "simplest in any single series." What made this movement of thought possible, and hence united the absolute and relative facts, was a conception of simple essences and deductions from them as primarily relational and not generic.[10] That is, a simple essence was the relation that established the constructive principle of an entire series of deductions. Descartes gave this a strictly mathematical description: "For example, if it comes into my thought that the number 6 is twice 3, I may then ask what is twice 6, viz. 12; again perhaps I seek for the double of this, viz. 24, and again of this, viz. 48. Thus I may easily deduce that there is the same proportion between 3 and 6, as between 6 and 12, and likewise 12 and 24, and so on, and hence that the numbers 3, 6, 12, 24, 48, etc. are in continued proportion."[11] In this example the simple essence is the proportion or ratio, 2 to 1, which can be readily intuited. Once intuited, the ratio is established for all remaining numbers in the series. Possessing this principle of relation, the mind can discover any number or "fact" that falls in the same series, in this case the series, n, $2n$, $4n$, $8n$, ... The sense of order assumed in the operations of multiplication that established this geometric series is the "natural and correlative order" marked by intervals of "greater, less, or equal," a natural order of increasing magnitude.

Descartes claimed that reflection upon this sense of order gave him the "form involved by all questions that can be propounded about proportions or relations of things, and the order in which they should be investigated." He further asserted that this discovery embraced "the entire science of Pure Mathematics."[12] Indeed, all knowledge, other than the "simple and naked intuition" of essences, involved comparing objects (marking the "interval"), an activity that was practically the whole task set before reason.[13] New knowledge therefore must be brought into relation with existing knowledge by means of new comparisons. Comparisons implied the recognition of a common term, for one could recognize the relation of any two numbers "only by considering some third thing, namely unity, which is the common measure of both."[14] And not only was "unity" a common measure, a unit, it was also an assumption of continuity and completeness that made possible the assemblages of units that marked specific series of cognitions under examination: "It is also necessary to know that thanks to an assumed *unité*, continuous magnitudes can be reduced to a multiplicity."[15] In this citation Descartes perceived continuity as spatial, with *unité* referring to the continuity of lines and figures, an expression, one scholar has suggested, that indicates his primary concern for geometry over algebra.[16] The significance of the passage nonetheless lies with his insistence on treating spatial magnitudes as a problem of order and not simply of measurement. Linear continua were to be expressed and manipulated by numerical units in proportions, series, ratios, and so forth, all of which assumed corresponding arithmetic continua. Descartes thus joined an explicit grasp of continuity in the geometric sense with an accompanying implicit understanding of the ordinal notion of number (which Malebranche was later to make quite clear); and he recognized that specific, discrete series of cognitions were elicited from this continuity.[17]

Two additional observations corroborate the assertion that Descartes' sense of order was in close accord with features of the ordinal concept of number. The first concerns his use of the term "induction," which in the *Rules* was given three distinct meanings.[18] Descartes used it first as a synonym for complete "enumeration of the steps in a proof," and, second, in a more general manner to signify inference from "various and disconnected facts." But, third, and most significantly, the concept was also given a clearly mathematical denotation: "If . . . I wish to show by enumeration that the area of a circle is greater than the area of all other figures whose perimeter is equal, there is no need for me to call in review all other figures; it is enough to demonstrate this of certain others in particular, in order to get thence by induction the same conclusion about the others."[19] Because the number of sides on a plane figure could be increased ad infinitum from a three-sided figure to a four-sided one, to five-sided, and so on, it would be impossible to complete the "enumeration" by examining all of them— impossible and needless. To prove the theorem one need only establish that the area of a circle exceed the area of a triangle and a square, both of whose perimeters equal the circumference of the circle. For what is true of n (three-sided figure) and $n+1$ (four-sided figure) must be true of the entire number realm, and therefore any polygon of p sides. Again, Descartes treated a geometric problem in a manner that assumed the continutiy of the number realm—in this case by utilizing mathematical induction and its implied principle of recurrence.

The second point takes us beyond the *Rules* themselves. There Descartes had referred to two distinct but closely related orders: the order exhibited by the "facts" that were the objects of investigation; the order of thoughts in which an investigation should proceed. Reflection upon the former, he claimed, yielded the latter, and this was possible because the order of thoughts was identical to the order of numbers. In a revealing letter to Mersenne, written in 1629, Descartes was explicit about this identity. Discussing the possibility of a universal language, which would facilitate all philosophical disputes and make them manageable, he remarked that the basis for such a language would have to consist of "primitive words" and their symbols, arranged so that there would be "an order between all thoughts that can be contained in the mind, in the same way that there is [an order] naturally established between numbers."[20] Descartes' contention that this ideal language would be desirable indicates the degree to which he sought to identify the order of thoughts with the order of number, a goal not weakened by his awareness that creating and implementing such a language would be, practically speaking, quite impossible. The final step in Descartes' widening sense of order[21] was from the "order of thoughts" to the "order of reasons," the latter being often iterated as the keynote of his method. Again writing to Mersenne, this time in 1640:

It is to be observed in everything I write that I do not follow the order of subject matters but only that of reasons, that is to say, I do not undertake to say in one and the same place everything which belongs to a subject, because it would be impossible for me to prove it satisfactorily, . . . but in reasoning by order, *a facilioribus ad difficiliora*, I deduce thereby what I can, . . . which is . . . the true way of finding and explaining the truth.[22]

The order of reasons, once it reveals the principles of its own construction, makes it possible to follow any subject matter to whatever limits one desires. The order *a facilioribus ad difficiliora* was therefore a more general description of the same movement from simple essences to remoter chains of operations, or deductions, which he had described in the *Rules*. From the order of facts to the order of thoughts, to the order of reasons, a vision of intellectual relations suggested by the ordinal concept provided Descartes an archetype for comprehending natural order.[23]

Nor was this all; the cardinal concept was equally significant. As some scholars have indicated, Descartes placed considerable importance on the relation between thought and object, between idea and existent. A. G. A. Balz writes, for instance: "Knowledge means to him certainty. Certainty . . . means specificity of correlation between idea and existent."[24] Indeed the representational or copy theory of knowledge that matured in the seventeenth century focused primarily upon the correlation between idea and existent object as the key to the meaning of truth. An idea was true if it corresponded directly to an object existing outside of thought, a notion

Descartes articulated in yet another of his letters to Mersenne: "This word *truth*, in its proper meaning, describes the conformity of thought with object"[25] (object here referring to existent, not object of thought). The connection between the "conformity" of thought and object and the mathematical principle of correspondence lies in the tacit assumption of analytic geometry, that it is possible to "represent the points on a line, and therefore points in a plane and in space, by means of numbers."[26] The primary correspondence for Descartes was between the arithmetic and linear continua, alluded to earlier.[27] Although the definition of this correspondence was not made fully explicit until the famous Dedekind-Cantor axiom of the late nineteenth century,[28] Descartes relied on it implicitly and constantly in his conception of the relation between mind and matter. Only by assuming such a correlation could one know anything about matter.[29] Matter was simply that which was extended, and the various forms extension assumed could be represented to the "corporeal imagination" as geometric figures. Cognitions of those figures were possible only if the order of ideas that examined them corresponded to them, that is, if numbers corresponded to points, and hence to lines, planes, solids, and other geometric figures. Having struck upon this in his mathematical studies, Descartes realized that he had found the key to a unified science, thus destroying the separation of two genera—arithmetic (algebra by his time) and geometry, the former dealing with numbers and purely ideal intuitions of succession and relation, the latter dealing with magnitudes and perceptual intuitions of space. The mental construct of correspondence between these two realms was then incorporated into his own attempts to generalize about method, epistemology, and truth. Consequently, correspondence (or "conformity") became the basis for the connection between the realm of ideas and that of spaces, between ideas and matter, a connection underscored by the cardinal concept of number.

A brief description of the entire process of mathematical thinking given by Whitehead helps to clarify the above. In *Science and the Modern World*, he wrote that there are three important features that mark mathematical abstraction and its relation to the world of experience. There is first the initial abstraction, in which elements of reality are expressed in numerical language—the one-to-one correspondence of abstract units and real objects. Second, there are the manipulations of relations between units according to principles of operation that function strictly within the abstract realm of number, manipulations resulting in the creation—potentially infinite— of new relations. Finally there is the application of these new relations to reality through experiment, to test whether or not they do in fact correspond to the real world.[30] Since Descartes envisioned this procedure, it is not at all surprising to find him at times writing about ideas conforming to objects or about experiments, both of which are crucial for the movement from real experience to mathematical abstraction and back again. Some Cartesian scholars have noted this by emphasizing these two points of connection. Balz, for example, sees Descartes' central epistemic problem as abstracting from existents and how this is to be accomplished, [31] while Alan Gewirth stresses the return to the real world in the application of mathematical relations to experience, a "non-mathematical, or specifically physical, application of the method, wherein the center of consideration is not the general formal relations of intelligible essences, but those specific essences, and consequences thereof, which exist in the material universe."[32] For Descartes, therefore—and this was novel in epistemology—the process of mathematical reasoning proffered the basis for a description of both a new abstract order and the close affinity of that order with experience. The principle of recurrence (which as White-head indicated is the foundation of periodicity and hence of all physical theories seeking to establish laws for the periodic, or recurring, events of the phenomenal world) gave Descartes the model for a new order of ideas, the natural order of increasing magnitude, as well as the foundation for the discovery and formal construction of new knowledge within that order. The principle of correspondence provided him an insight into cor-relating knowledge with the phenomenal world, both at the point of initial abstraction and at the point of verification. In part explicitly, in part implicitly, Descartes effected a redefi-nition of knowledge, of the conceptual and real orders and the relation between them—a redefinition given its cohesion by the submerged model of 'number'.

Along with redefining the structure of thought and its rela-tion to experience, Descartes was compelled to describe anew the activity of thinking. On the model of 'substance', as seen earlier, that activity began with the intuition of "mental ex-tracts" from sensory experience, which resulted in the concept defined as a term. In the Middle Ages the mind was said to contain these concepts (*species*, *intentiones*) in contrast to "ideas" that were defined as the eternal archetypes contemplated only by God. Since archetypes were contemplated solely by God, the question of their external reference was left unasked. "God could create instances of one of his ideas, but his idea was in no way dependent upon the existence of such instances."[33] As E. J. Ashworth has written, Descartes' continual use of the word 'idea' indicated his desire to carry this implication to the realm of human cognitions, a desire that accorded nicely with his awareness that the meaning of number relations precluded any extrasystemic reference.[34] The word 'idea' then applied exclusively to the contents of the mind and avoided all sugges-tion that mental contents must depend causally upon the ex-ternal world.[35] As Descartes phrased it, the idea is the "form of any thought," with "thought" in this passage specifically excluding imagery.[36] Consequently, the activity that produced these ideas also had to be unrelated to the external world in any causal manner and thus comprised a pure intellectual spontaneity or, in Léon Brunschvicg's words, a "dynamism of mind."[37] For this reason Descartes redefined intuition as the activity that grasped not sensory extracts (although on occasion in his mechanics he did appear to use it in such a fashion[38]) but those simple essences or "natures" that he later called clear and distinct ideas.[39] Moreover, deduction, the second type of intellectual activity described by Descartes, was defined as the "necessary inference from other facts that are known with certainty"[40]—a definition that further explicated the sense of intellectual spontaneity devoid of external causality. Because, as Brunschvicg writes, "deduction only makes intuition explicit,"[41] it functions exclusively within the realm of clear and distinct ideas and furnishes the step by step movement in a series of cognitions. For Descartes then the activities of thinking were those that resulted in intuitive creations and deductive certainties: the mathematical mind at work on Poincaré's intuition of "pure number"!

Part of the fascination with which the historical Descartes has captivated scholarly audiences for generations rests in the fact that he did not simply harvest from mathematics new insights into the nature of science and epistemology, but sought also to incorporate these innovations into established philosophical traditions.[42] Significantly enough, throughout his life he seemed to recognize the models of both 'substance' and 'number' as fundamental. In the *Rules* he claimed that the intellect was capable of grasping "simple things" such as "existence, unity, duration and the like."[43] Some fifteen years later in a letter to Princess Elizabeth, he ventured the same opinion: "I observe that there are in us certain primitive notions which are as it were *models* on which all our other knowledge is patterned. There are very few such notions. First there are the most general ones, such as *being*, *number*, and *duration*, which apply to everything we can conceive."[44] When we recall that "unity" for Descartes was the foundation of "number," we see these statements as virtually identical in import.[45] In addition, "duration" as developed in his thought meant the continual recreation or bringing into existence in successive instants everything that is, an act performed by God.[46] Because successive instants of creation could be placed on a coordinate scale as a time axis and treated as a numerical continuum, duration was also subject to mathematical description. It was therefore infused with both the notions of existence and number and could be accounted for by these two more general categories. Without being too reductionist here, we can interpret these passages as Descartes' apparent recognition of two "primitive notions"— "being" (or substance) and "number"—that were the most fundamental "models" for all that could be known. And while he did not conceive these notions as incompatible, there are in his writings chains of reasons from each that reveal an historical tension between the old and new archetypes.

Descartes' definition of substance and its place in his metaphysics confirm his continuing attachment to scholastic tradition. Although in the *Rules* he had denied the incommunicability of the genera as an epistemic principle, when he turned his attention to ontological issues the axiom that a substance could not be anything other than simple, discrete, and incommunicable, "a thing which so exists that it needs no other thing in order to exist,"[47] assumed major significance. Strictly speaking, only one substance met this criterion—God.[48] But the term, Descartes claimed, also signified things created by God, of which there were two kinds, mental and material. With this latter assertion Descartes echoed Aristotle's meaning of substance, defining it as "everything . . . by means of which there exists anything that we perceive, i.e. any property, quality, or attribute, of which we have a real idea" (or in other words, a substratum of which all else is predicated).[49] It was in short the definition of a generic concept. And although the actual substances were reduced to two (Descartes claimed that God could not be considered as a substance univocally with mind and matter[50]), all the parts of reality had to be classified into one or the other of these categories, a requirement reminiscent of abstract thought characterized by genus and species.

Closely related to his understanding of substance was Descartes' acceptance of the traditional meaning of cause, which was inherited from ancient and scholastic sources and which was widely shared by his contemporaries, including his Jesuit instructors at *La Fleche*.[51] To cause something meant to bring that something into existence, a process that implied as much reality in the cause as in the effect, since something could not be created from nothing.[52] Descartes' subscription to this theory, often referred to as "transitive causality,"[53] has already been alluded to in mentioning his treatment of duration. His description of motion serves to elaborate the point. Because matter and space were identified with each other (space was simply the place occupied by matter), motion was defined as a body's change of place, a change that occurred instantaneously.[54] When a piece of matter was moved from one place to another, a second piece instantly assumed the former's place, preventing what would have otherwise been a void. It followed that the amount of motion in the universe remained constant since every displacement resulted in other instantaneous displacements. The problem then was how to account for the existence of motion in its entirety. It had to be brought into being not only at the beginning of the universe in time but at each successive instant, and the only agency that could render this possible was an omnipotent God. The acts of creation and conservation were thus identical; it was God's continual activity as transitive creator, or cause, that kept the world moving.[55]

Descartes never abandoned this reliance upon transitive causality. Time and again he repeated that what is true is what exists, and what is false is that which does not exist; for if something had not really been created, we would not be able to perceive its essence.[56] Nor did he surrender his urge to classify. It was reality brought into being generically as mind or matter that unfolded itself in its essence as thought or extension before the cognitions of man. But, as Brunschvicg has persuasively argued, despite Descartes' acknowledgment of scholastic teachings on cause and substance, his handling of these doctrines produced some aggravated and confusing results. To begin with, the notion of substance had customarily carried two important corollaries in the Middle Ages. The first was the juxtaposition of the multiplicity of substances,[57] all derivable causally from being-in-general (a multiplicity of classes that Descartes reduced to two). The second involved the "division of a unique being, such as man, into a body and a soul equally materialised by the imagination of a common border."[58] In Descartes' thought these two corollaries clashed head on. For like St. Thomas he sought to affirm the substantial union of body and soul[59] but, in so doing, was forced to a disjunction that he never fully acknowledged. On the one hand, if man were a substantial union between soul and body, he would then be an "*ens per se*" and as such not composed accidentally of two heterogeneous substances. It would follow that soul and body would be incomplete in themselves, and only when brought together could they constitute an essential being, the complete substance of man. Yet, on the other hand, Descartes denied that soul and body were incomplete substances; as he consistently reiterated, each was capable of standing by itself and serving as the ontological host of countless predicates. This condition was impossible for St. Thomas who believed that if man were to be substantially whole, the parts of his composition could not be. Elsewise man would be only an accident.[60]

Beyond this unresolved dichotomy in Descartes' conception of substance, the *cogito*[61] and its concomitant proof of God's existence (which together comprised the heart of Descartes' metaphysics and one of the most succinct and recondite of philosophical formulations) reveal even more clearly the tension between tradition and innovation in his thought. With the phrases "I think, therefore I am"[62] and "I exist, therefore God exists,"[63] he sought to describe two complex relationships: between thought and being; between man and God. His manner of considering these relations, as has been implied in the foregoing, departed markedly from the syllogistic expression of the scholastics, a departure Descartes expressed unmistakably in a letter to Clerselier: "This author [Gassendi] supposes that knowledge of particular propositions must always be deduced from universals, following the order of the syllogisms of dialectic—in this he displays how little he knows of the way truth must be sought."[64] But although his approach to truth in metaphysical matters lay outside the syllogistic form, it was not unaffected by considerations inherent in the model of 'substance'. Evidence for this is found in the parallel inferences from "I think" to "I am" and from the idea of God to His existence. The *cogito* was prima facie a statement uniting two senses of "I." The first of these was "I" in its objective connotation, seen in the created object of thought, "I think"; the latter was "I" as subject, initiator or creator of mental objects. The idea, "I think," for Descartes, presupposed its being created or brought into being by a mental activity that necessarily existed —hence "I am."[65] It is significant that Descartes immediately attached the term "substance" to his perception of the inference between "I think" and "I am": "From that ['I think, therefore I am'] I knew that I was a substance the whole essence or nature of which is to think."[66] In so doing, he accomplished two things. First, he gave ideas an ontological status in the generic category of mental objects; ideas were not relations per se but modifications of the thinking substance. Thus Descartes responded to the implicit question, What is it to be an idea? This type of question was central to the epistemology and metaphysics of Aristotle and scholastics. Second, he relied upon the conception of transitive causality in claiming that mental substance created or brought into being mental objects and therefore had to contain as much reality as the ideas it produced, again echoing traditional thinking.

Descartes made these same appeals when he inferred God's existence from His perfection. Arguments supporting this inference had been familiar to St. Thomas and the majority of scholastics, but they had been construed on the Aristotelian supposition that it is impossible to pursue to infinity a series of essentially ordered causes. Since it was held that in the material world essences of things, and hence their causes, differed according to the degree of ontological perfection possessed by their structures, it followed that one could pass upward through the generic hierarchy from specificity in nature to universality in mind, and ultimately to the ontologically necessary and perfect first cause—God. As we have seen, Descartes abandoned the hierarchical structure upon which scholastic arguments rested. Particular causation in the physical world was only 'accidentally' ordered, and progress to infinity was always possible either in thought or extension; that is, number and matter were infinitely divisible or extendable. Nonetheless it remained certain in principle that thought, matter, and duration had to be created in the aggregate sense (just as with motion); God must then exist as the essential cause of all that is. Descartes' reasoning behind this was the same he employed with the *cogito*. From the objective idea of God, one could infer that the real substance of God was necessary to produce the idea, just as from the objective idea of oneself, "I think," one could infer the "substantial I." And because the objective idea of God was infinite perfection, which contained all that is in thought and matter, it followed that God existed as perfect substance, since any cause had to possess as much reality as its effect.[67] Brunschvicg summarizes: "The sole proof that results really in the existence of God is the one that seeks the cause of the idea of perfect and infinite being that is in us; for this cause of an objective reality, perfect and infinite, can itself only be perfect and infinite."[68]

From the idea of perfection, Descartes developed a second and related proof of God's existence. Briefly stated, since it was God's essence to be perfect and since His perfection included His existing, it followed that He necessarily existed. That is, God could not be separated from actually existing any more than the idea of a mountain could be separated from that of a valley.[69] Heading off what was to become later a fundamental criticism of this "ontological proof"—the claim that adding 'existing' to God was simply adding one idea to another, not establishing God's actual being—Descartes argued that, while it was true that one could not prove the existence of a mountain or valley from the fact that they could not be separated in thought, with God the case was different. He really did exist, not because of necessary relations between ideas, but because of the "necessity which lies in the thing itself, i.e. the necessity of the existence of God determines me [Descartes] to think this way."[70] In short, a reality—prior to thought ontologically speaking—imposes itself upon thought, and the thought that thinks God is the thought that conceives this reality apart from the constituents of reason. Containing generically all that is in thought or matter, the objective idea of perfection thus presupposed for Descartes an ontologically prior and determining substance. This assumption lay at the heart of scholastic and Aristotelian thought and was a corner-stone of the model of 'substance'.

Yet the *cogito* formulation implied as well another kind of abstraction. Beginning with man's own thought, Descartes worked his way back to God solely through intellectual relations between ideas, not, as had St. Thomas, through causal relations between ideas and nature. And the order of ideas, as has been indicated, involved no generic categories or ontological priorities but relations of the kind defined by 'number' and mathematics, whose meaning implicitly excluded extra-systemic references. This understanding, when expressed in the *cogito*, suggested the image of man as a unit of thought, a suggestion reiterated in one of Descartes' later letters. Writing to Mesland about the meaning of the phrase "body of a man," Descartes claimed that, when referring to material body in general, one meant a "determinate part of matter, a part of the quantity of which the universe is composed."[71] If the quantity of matter were to change, so would the body; it would be, in his words, "no longer numerically the same" body or piece of matter. However, the phrase "body of a man," he contended, meant not just a determinate part of matter but something more, "the whole of the matter joined to the soul of that man." As long as the man's body remained joined in substantial union with the soul (a union created and conserved by God), the body remained "numerically the same body," even though the quantity of matter might alter. Human bodies, he summed up, were from birth "numerically the same because they are informed by the same soul."[72] It was the soul, or mind, that perceived the *unité* enabling the body attached to it to remain the same in its "numerical sense." This description could have meant only that man was in essence an *unité*—both unit and unity—of thought. Insofar as the *cogito* had established the objective existence of the ego in the idea "I think," that existence was as a clear and distinct idea, a simple essence that was perceived through intuition.

But since a unit of thought or simple essence was primarily a relation and not a genus or species, it followed that a relation was inherent in the intuition of the unitary idea of an objective "I." This relation was the movement of thought from imperfection to perfection. The objective "I" was imperfect because of the doubt that produced it, and an imperfect thought implied a perfect thought. The inference, however, was not one of strict, logical contradiction, since imperfection was not the logical antithesis of perfection. Rather, imperfection rested on a continuum of increasing magnitude, extending from infinite perfection at one terminus to infinite imperfection at the other—a continuum marked by the relations greater, equal, or less that attended clear and distinct ideas. Further, it was not only on the order of objective ideas that the connection between imperfection and perfection was maintained. This same continuum provided the grounds for inferring from the substantial, creative "I" to the existing perfect substance, God. Descartes proffered this view in the *Meditations*, placing his own being on a progression of perfections that ranged from infinity (God) to himself as imperfect being, to a "certain negative idea of nothing," that which is "infinitely removed from any kind of perfection."[73] Perfection and imperfection then were conceived on the order of purely ideal relations, that is, solely within the realm of mathematical intelligence or in Brunschvicg's phrase, as the "consciousness of intuitive *unité*."

To sum up the foregoing, Descartes relied on abstractions formulated according to the model of 'number' to describe man's relation to God. He insisted that the intuition of the "Cogito" was inseparable from the nature of reason and therefore attested to the infinity within us:[74] "Also, in pausing long enough on this meditation [the *cogito*], one gradually acquires a very clear, and if I may so speak, an intuitive knowledge of intellectual nature in general, the idea of which, being considered without limitation, is what God represents to us, and, limited, is that of an angel or a human soul."[75] This order, based on pure intelligence, existed both within the realm of intelligence (objective ideas) and within the realm of being (the creative substances that produced ideas). Again, Brunschvicg's incisive observation: "After having elicited the divine infinity of the *Cogitatio* from the *Cogito*, he turns back to the *Sum* to elicit the divine absolute of being."[76] On the other hand it was the tendency to form abstractions on the basis of 'substance' that led Descartes to conceive the ontological status of the "I" as a thinking substance that created or brought into being objective ideas, as well as enabling him to move from the idea of God as perfection to the existence of God as perfect and creative substance.

These two tendencies in Descartes' thought produced a tension that was to underscore the problems faced by two generations of his successors and indeed was ultimately to lead to the downfall of many facets of Cartesianism.[77] Even with Descartes himself, the conflict had begun to emerge, as witnessed in his ambiguous treatment of the critical term "infinity." Following the model of 'number', infinity in its mathematical sense signified the mental acts of extrapolating or interpolating from the order of thoughts, or ideal relations, acts that could recur without determinable end—ad infinitum. Infinity in this sense was thus privative, and when ascribed to God it meant that God was necessary or assumed in human thought, even though thought could not conceive God in a positive sense. At times Descartes utilized this meaning of infinity in describing how man could know God. One passage from a letter to Regius is particularly clear: "You [Regius] say that it is because we have in ourselves some degree of wisdom and power and goodness that we form the idea of an infinite, or at least indefinite, degree of wisdom and power and goodness and the other attributes of God; just as it is because we have some degree of quantity that we form the idea of infinite quantity. I entirely agree, and am quite convinced that we have no idea of God except one formed in this manner."[78] Just as the principle of recurrence functioned within mathematics to introduce infinity into the number realm, so did that same principle serve to bring the idea of an infinite God into relation with man. God was thus not believed in but was recognized as assumptive, an integral part of man's own intelligence, a necessary presupposition for the acquisition of any knowledge.

Yet Descartes was quite aware that this conception of God was clearly at odds with traditional views, and he prudently introduced a distinction between "indefinite" and "infinite" to preserve the traditional metaphysical predicates of God.[79] "Indefinite" was to be applied to all of those conceptions that issued from human thought and that admitted of no conceivable end. For example, matter was indefinitely extended and divisible, because the mind could conceive no possible limitations to either extension or divisibility: "When I say that matter is indefinitely extended, I am saying that it extends further than anything a human being can conceive. None the less, I think there is a very great difference between the vastness of this bodily extension and the vastness of God's extension, or rather not extension, since strictly He has none, but substance or essence; and so I call the latter simply infinite, and the former indefinite."[80] "Infinite" applied to the substance of God, referring to the positive perfections that God could be said to possess. Furthermore, one could by natural reason know those positive perfections, know that God is "all good, all powerful, and all truthful."[81] On this reading of infinity, man's imperfection was not the starting point but a derivation from the infinite possessions attributed to God: "I say that the notion I have of the infinite is in me before that of the finite because, by the mere fact that I conceive being or that which is, without thinking whether it is finite or infinite, what I conceive is infinite being; but in order to conceive a finite being, I have to take something away from this general notion of being, which must accordingly be there first."[82] In contrast to God as assumptive, this passage described God in an intuitive manner.[83] God was intuited as a metaphysical being, with all His infinitely perfect attributes, and as existing apart from and prior to human conceptions. This existence was shown to be ontologically possible and necessary not because of 'number' but because of 'substance' and cause.

The passage of thought from privative to positive infinity became one of the most critical inferences that Descartes bequeathed to the second half of the seventeenth century, not only for Cartesians, but for other philosophers, scientists, and theologians as well. It was often invoked in the attempt to unify the gradually emerging scientific epistemology and the traditional tenets of religious belief. Once proving the assumptive necessity of infinity—and thus God—for mathematical science, it became easy, comforting, and completely gratuitous for Descartes and others to think that they had established with equal certainty the God of Moses and Christ, the God who possessed positive, metaphysical attributes and who worked through a special, as well as a natural or general, revelation. The inference in short was founded not upon its own logical coherence but upon an unconscious shift in archetypes from 'number' to 'substance'.

Beyond the problem of infinity, the tension between these models in Cartesian thought was to host a number of critical intellectual dilemmas. Did "necessity" refer philosophically to a relation between ideas in the mathematical meaning, or did it involve the relation between being, and/or nature, and ideas? If the distinction was to be upheld, on what criteria was it based? Resolution of the ontological issue of connecting mind to matter and the epistemic distinction between primary and secondary qualities depended in no small part upon the connotations supplied to this term. Second, was science to be concerned with concepts that were relational and quantitative or with generic terms that described qualities and forces? For some the latter prolonged outmoded scholastic expressions such as that of 'dormitive powers causing sleep,' while others saw the former as restrictive in methodology and intention. Within religion the question emerged in the rivalry between assumptive and intuitive beliefs. General revelation or miracles and grace—how, if at all, were these to be united? Finally, there was the conflict between science and religion itself, between reason and faith, knowing and believing—how were these to be reconciled? If one could know only a mathematical god, how could he believe miracles that contravened the mathematical order? If God were only an assumption, an hypothesis, then how could one know Him as the living God? How could one "see clearly" as a natural philosopher and "believe blindly" as a Christian? For Nicolas Malebranche, who sought to fuse the achievements of Descartes with traditional Catholic Christianity, to fuse science and religion, responding to these and related issues was to constitute his life's work.

CHAPTER 3

'Number':
The Theory of Truth

The tension between 'substance' and 'number', largely submerged in Descartes' writings, surfaced more openly in the
thought of his most noted successor, Nicolas Malebranche.[1]
Our task will be to describe the manner in which Malebranche
refined and made more explicit this polarity of submerged
models and to indicate how the tension between these patterns
of thought affected his grasp of the relation between science
and religion. To achieve this end it is necessary to distinguish
between the epistemological and metaphysical descriptions that
Malebranche gave to some of his key concepts, even while
recognizing that the two modes of description were closely
interwoven and often indistinguishable in his own thinking.
As will be discussed later, he considered ideas, for example, as
real objects ontologically, real objects that served an epistemic
function essential to cognition. With this precaution in mind,
the advantage of discussing epistemic descriptions apart from
metaphysical ones is that the historian can more readily ascer-

tain the structural dilemmas surrounding innovation and tradition in Malebranche's thought. We shall be able to perceive more clearly both how and to what extent he sought to incorporate new insights derived from mathematics into the discourse of science, philosophy, and natural theology, as well as the manner in which these new insights accorded or conflicted with established and traditional modes of intellectual endeavor.

The principal contention of this and the following chapter is that the model of 'number' provides the historian with a central clue for an appreciation of Malebranche's epistemology and theory of science. Three threads of examination will bear this out. The first, considered in this chapter, is that the assumptions and inferences suggested by cardinal and ordinal concepts of number provide the structural framework for a proper understanding of Malebranche's theory of truth as relational and with it his rules for methodically attaining truth. The second and third lines of inquiry, appearing in the next chapter, will examine Malebranche's epistemological description of ideas and the concept of intelligible extension, his most mature expression of the 'number' model.

It bears repeating as a qualification that Malebranche was not totally conscious of eliciting his epistemology from the implications of 'number' even though the assumptions and inferences of 'number' are more easily discernible in his thought than in that of Descartes. A distinction merits introduction between Malebranche's explicit theory of mathematics and the implicit manner in which mathematics functioned in his epistemology as a "paradigm of knowledge."[2] Two Malebranche scholars, Paul Schrecker and André Robinet, have produced several valuable studies assessing the former, focusing on his philosophy of mathematics, his differences with Leibniz over the nature and significance of algebra vis-à-vis geometry, and his reception of and contribution to the study of calculus.[3]

Schrecker has even suggested that because Malebranche's "point of systematic departure is mathematics," one must "consider Malebranchean philosophy as the first coherent theory of modern mathematics."[4] Yet in intellectual history it is not solely these conscious ideas that interest us but also the shadow world between intuition and conscious expression. We may even acknowledge as a further guideline that principles and rules of method seldom, if ever, exist by themselves as starting points in the search for truths but are related to and derived from an underlying vision of the sorts of truths one seeks. The intention of the present chapters is thus to build on the findings of Robinet, Schrecker, and others and to see how Malebranche was led by 'number' to introduce a series of specific questions, definitions, and propositions as a basis for his epistemology— even though occasionally his conscious philosophy of mathematics appeared to lead him in an opposite direction. In this manner it is possible to substantiate, at least in the case of the Oratorian, Cassirer's comment cited earlier that mathematics increasingly became a moving force in Western thought.

Like Descartes, Malebranche adamantly rejected the scholastic theory of knowledge and its methods for deriving terms, use of dialectic, and adherence to syllogistic demonstration as the principal form of reasoning. Not only in his major work, *Recherche de la vérité*, but throughout his life, a twofold purpose motivated much of Malebranche's intellectual career: he sought to provide continued and trenchant criticism of scholastic epistemology, and concurrently to articulate a new understanding of science, method, and order as the foundation for that criticism. Excessive reliance upon tradition, he charged, had fostered intellectual errors that were the "cause of the mind's greatest disorder."[5] There was no clear and distinct idea of nature, nor of essence, nor indeed of any of the "general terms of logic" as traditionally conceived.[6] In the *Entretiens sur la*

métaphysique it is Ariste's insistence on "thinking in these abstract forms of genera and species" that impedes his understanding of truth.[7] To expunge 'substance' from our thinking
was the first step in alleviating the "mind's disorder."

Malebranche challenged the traditional way of thinking at
its two most vulnerable points with a sharp critique of syllogistic logic and an offensive against the reliance upon sensation
that was required for the derivation of terms employed by
such a logic. Syllogistic demonstrations, he conceded, possessed an aesthetic attractiveness, but their cognitive value was
minimal because reasoning based upon "substantial forms" did
not serve to discover anything new nor to express with any
greater clarity what was already known. When, for instance,
philosophers used such "beautiful words as genus, species, act,
potency, nature, form, faculties, qualities, cause by self, cause
by accident," they sought to explain things but "without having any knowledge of them."[8] Technically such terms and
demonstrations were not incorrect; who would dare deny the
proposition that "fire dissolves metals because it possesses the
dissolving faculty?" But although "such or similar manners of
speaking are not false" in a technical sense, in effect "they
mean nothing."[9] Such modes of speaking and thinking were,
in short, trivial. While this sort of attack on scholastic logic in
the seventeenth century was by no means unique to Malebranche,[10] his was one of the sharper and more thorough
expressions of it. Moreover, he steadfastly maintained this
attitude throughout his life; witness a letter to Père André in
1709: "I have nothing to say to you about logic. I know
nothing good about it except the natural [logic] joined to the
rules I presented in the 6th book of the *Recherche de la vérité*. I
have never made use of what has been taught me about syllogisms. A little good sense and attention discovers when an argument is good for nothing."[11] Good sense and attention: these

were the proper substitutes for the logic of Aristotle which occupied "the mind too much" and diverted the mind from "the attention it should bring to the subjects it examines."[12]

Indeed, good sense and attention enabled one to understand the second and more significant shortcoming of traditional logic, its excessive reliance upon the vague and undetermined ideas that were derived from the senses.[13] In this criticism Malebranche echoed Descartes' position that sensations did not represent objects outside the mind but were simply mental modifications (of which more later). Accordingly, Aristotle and his medieval followers, whom Malebranche unceremoniously lumped together as schoolmen and philosophers, erred when they claimed that the terms elicited from sensations provided objective knowledge of things in nature. Their error was twofold. First, they moved from the perception of a quality in something, such as heat in fire, to the contention that such qualities were a part of the "manners of being" of the thing itself. This inference was completely false because it confused the subjective or purely mental fact of perception with the objective or extra-mental reality of the thing perceived.[14] Second, the schoolmen failed to see how the uncertainty and deceptiveness of the individual senses led inexorably to the complete subjectivity and unreliability of sensation in general. In many passages throughout his works, Malebranche contended that to discover truths one needs first to grasp the cause of errors, and the chief cause of error lay in the frailty of sensations. Consequently, the ideas derived from sensations (terms, as here described in Chapter 1) were equally frail and deceptive, and all generic relations based upon such terms must be subject to doubt.[15]

In singling out the senses and the mind's "readiness . . . to take up abstract natures and general ideas of logic for those that are real and particular,"[16] Malebranche assailed what he saw as the two most seductive sources of error in traditional epistemology. He pursued this attack systematically in the first five books of the *Recherche*, exposing in order the errors that resulted from misuse of the various mental faculties—the sensations, the imagination, the understanding, the inclinations, and the passions.[17] In the process he gradually revealed the basis for his critique which then was summarized in the sixth and final book, "De la methode," as the culmination of his thought. There he made clear his reliance on Descartes' rules of method, both from the *Rules* and from the *Discourse*, and showed even more explicitly their relation to mathematics and 'number' as the model for scientific knowledge.[18]

The goal of Descartes' method had been to unify all the sciences into a single concept of "human wisdom." Similarly, Malebranche's chief aim was to establish a "universal science," which postulated a single body of knowledge that communicated all genera according to common principles, rules of method, and an apprehension of mathematical order. Knowledge of such a general science would yield the basis for knowledge in all the particular sciences and render those who knew how to make use of it "savants" in the true sense of the term.[19] This true science was to be found in developing the mind's "capacity for judging soundly all things that are suited to it."[20] The first and most general principle governing such judgments incorporated the Cartesian principle of doubt: "One must never give complete assent except to propositions that appear so evidently true that one cannot deny them without feeling an inner pain and the secret reproaches of reason."[21] One must doubt—that is, withhold assent from—all propositions that were not clear and distinct to the inner light of reason. Precipitous assent to propositions was in fact the most grievous cause of error and a poor use of man's liberty. Man must reason only about those truths of which he has clear and distinct ideas, Malebranche reiterated elsewhere, to conserve "evidence" in reasoning.[22] Since evidence referred to clear and distinct ideas linked in chains of reasoning, Malebranche followed with a corollary principle, stating again with Descartes that one ought to begin with the most simple truths and progress slowly to the more complex.[23] His two most general principles of knowledge thus indicated that universal science was to be derived from truths discovered gradually and secured only through the mind's assenting to the correct evidence represented by clear and distinct ideas.

To guide the mind's assent, Malebranche outlined six specific rules for systematic inquiry into truth. Rule one states it is necessary to conceive distinctly the sort of question one proposes to resolve and to fix clearly the terms and parameters of the problem in order to "recognize in this manner the relations one seeks." Second, if these relations cannot be readily identified, then there is a need for one or more "middle ideas" to serve as a "common measure" by which the unknown truths sought can be brought into conceptual relationship with the original terms of the problem. Rules three and four state respectively that all elements not essential to difficult problems must be eliminated and that, once a difficult problem is properly reduced, it is necessary to divide the subject of meditation into parts and consider such parts successively, "according to the *natural order*, beginning with the simplest."[24] Scholars have noted the similarity of these rules to Descartes' four rules of method outlined in the *Discourse*.[25] Beyond this similarity their formulation suggests that Malebranche was intimately familiar with the *Rules* as well.[26] Rules three and four above, for example, mirror the phrasing of Descartes' rule five, which stipulates the need to "reduce involved and obscure propositions step by step to those that are simpler."[27] More to the point, Malebranche's concern with a "common measure," often essential for establishing the relation between two ideas, reflected directly Descartes' insistence in rule fourteen that unity was the common measure between two terms of a relation.[28]

This internal evidence indicates that Malebranche was fully aware of Descartes' perception of unity as a basis for order as he had implied in the *Rules*, a unity that joined geometry and algebra and that provided the groundwork for the more general rules of method. In fact the rules in the *Discourse* do not include explicit reference to the importance of intermediary terms or common measures, and it was the implications of this rule in particular, as we shall see, that enabled Malebranche to tie general methodological considerations directly to mathematical order through his concept of *unité*.

Malebranche's final two rules were linked closely and deliberately to the procedures of algebra. Rule five was a rule of convenience. One ought to abridge his ideas and "then arrange them in his imagination or write them on paper" so that one can employ his mental faculties with economy.[29] This was drawn from the apparent advantages of algebraic notation. Fully symbolized by this time, an algebraic expression provided the most succinct manner of designating a mathematical relation. One need not define a circle rhetorically as a plane figure whose perimeter is everywhere equidistant from a point called the center when $a^2 + b^2 = c^2$ says the same thing. Moreover the latter is far more abbreviated and manipulable than the rhetorical definition. In rule six Malebranche stated generally that all ideas, once clearly established, ought to be compared by "the rules of combinations." By this he meant the manipulation of relationships in an equation, reduction of complex fractions, transposition of terms, indication of identities, and other combinations and procedures proper to algebra. Should all these operations fail to establish the relation sought, Malebranche claimed it would be necessary to begin anew, isolating the terms, relating them through "middle ideas," reducing complex problems, analysing their components, and performing further operations in the mind and "on paper."[30] It was never his contention that one need consciously follow all six rules at all times in the pursuit of truth. Rather they were conceived as guides for instruction, for the development of mental habits that were natural and proportioned to the mind. Once one became accustomed to asking the types of questions suggested by the rules, he would abandon most, if not all, of the fruitless efforts of generic thinking, those mental habits based on 'substance' which divided and fragmented the mind's labors. "In a word, they [rules] can regulate the mind's attention without dividing it."[31]

Unquestionably Malebranche himself saw clearly that mathematical reasoning underlay these rules and provided the proper means for developing new mental habits and for establishing the criteria with which to criticize scholasticism. His early formation as a Cartesian, notes Gouhier, involved extensive study of mathematics, both for its mental discipline and as the key to understanding the new science.[32] Yet his conception of mathematics differed from that of Descartes, who, despite joining algebra and geometry, continued to grant the latter a primary role. In Brunschvicg's interpretation Descartes' mathematics stressed the "application of algebra to geometry"[33] and left intact the prevalence of the intuition of spatial magnitude while minimizing the intuition of number.[34] With Malebranche, on the other hand, the intuition of number carried the day and resulted in the "reduction of geometry to algebra."[35] There were several reasons for this apparent shift from Descartes' view to Malebranche's. Malebranche agreed with Descartes that "all the exact sciences can be related to geometry," but he went on to point out that geometry was simply the most exalted use of imagination and did not represent in itself pure conceptualization.[36] Geometers relied on lines, figures, planes, solids, and other graphic constructions to conduct their investigations, and all these were intelligible only when taken in through sight. Because geometric figurings rested on one of the senses, they were subject to error. A line, for example, is defined as having no width and is thus invisible. One's quill, it follows, could never be sharp enough to achieve absolute exactitude. Geometry was useful, to be sure, for all problems of mechanics could be expressed sensibly through the use of lines and figures,[37] and with respect to bodies in nature it should be considered an "abstract" discipline. But it remained nonetheless sensible vis-à-vis pure conception. The major limitation was the all too frequent failure of geometers to recognize that their graphic representations were only a useful half-way measure in the search for truth, not the end of the quest.

Consequently, Malebranche turned to arithmetic and algebra, and later on, after its discovery, to calculus in order to describe what he perceived as a purely conceptual model of truth. Unsullied by a sensory spatial content, arithmetic and algebra (which he understood correctly as arithmetic generalized) together provided "the true logic that serves to discover truth and to produce in the mind all the extension of which it is capable."[38] This logic was pure, not constructed from imagination or sensation; its exactitude was incontestable; no wide ink marks could mitigate the truth of $a^2+b^2=c^2$ as defining a circle. In identifying algebra with true logic itself, Malebranche deemed it the key to all other sciences: "Analysis, or spatial algebra, is assuredly the most beautiful, I mean the most fruitful and certain of all sciences. Without it the mind has neither penetration nor extension; and with it the mind is capable of knowing nearly all that can be known with certitude and evidence. . . . In a word, it is a universal science, and as such the key to all other sciences."[39] The structure and operations of mathematics provided for the discovery of new truths through the use of equations in isolating and finding unknowns and assured that the truths discovered were logically rigorous and certain. Indeed, mathematics was not merely the key to other sciences; it was scientific knowledge par excellence.[40]

The mind structured knowledge of nature in the same fashion that it functioned mathematically. The rules of method therefore were designed to encourage and facilitate this activity, for only thus could the mind assent to those "real relations," the truths proportioned to its capacity.

To understand the theory of truths as real relations we must examine the concepts 'relation' and 'real'. For heuristic purposes we shall distinguish them at present, examining here the theory of relations and in a later chapter the theory of reality. Malebranche claimed that in general all truths could be called "real relations," and he characterized relations with at least four different sets of categories. In the *Recherche* his initial discussion of relations rested on a distinction between necessity and contingency. Those truths or relations that were "immutable by their nature" and had been decreed by the will of God were typed as necessary; all others were contingent. Of necessary truths, mathematics, metaphysics, and "even a large part of physics and morality" were exemplary. History, grammar, particular law or custom, and other subjects that depended on the changing will or sensations of men fell to the lot of contingent truths.[41] Later in the *Recherche* he introduced a second division, this between "relations of magnitude" and "relations of quality." Relations of magnitude carried the identifying feature of "more or less"; those of quality were simply all others not accountable by exact degrees.[42] Elsewhere, he wrote of a third set of categories, similar to the second, distinguishing between relations of "magnitude" and relations of "perfection."[43] (Discussion of "quality" and "perfection" will follow in Chapter 5.) Finally Malebranche frequently employed yet a fourth manner of describing relations, a tripartite division: relations between different things; between ideas and things; and between ideas and ideas.[44] Paraphrasing him, an example of the first is 'the earth is larger than the moon'; of the second, 'there is a sun and the idea of a sun'; of the third,

'$2+2=4$'.[45] Although this latter description of truths utilized three classes, whereas the first three sets of categories were in pairs, Malebranche added that all relations involving created objects in nature, either relations between things or between things and ideas, were contingent, uncertain, and inexact[46]— vis-à-vis by implication necessary, certain, and exact. Consequently, the latter description also reduced relations to a bifurcation of classes. (As if four classifications were not enough, Malebranche also stated that all relations were either equal or unequal, and further that equality and inequality were either exact and certain, on the one hand, or inexact and uncertain, on the other. The former, exact equalities and inequalities, applied to relations of magnitude; the latter to relations between things or between things and ideas.[47]) Underlying these numerous descriptions of relations Malebranche envisioned truths of two basic sorts, quite in keeping with the seventeenth century's growing concern for separating primary and secondary qualities in nature. Primary truths, those sought by natural philosophy, were quantitative, necessary, and purely conceptual, existing between ideas. These were the relations of magnitude required for an exact knowledge of nature. Secondary truths comprised loosely everything that was left over. Variously described as qualities, perfections, contingent relations, or sensory relations involving created objects in nature, they were inexact and uncertain. At best they yielded a lowly practical knowledge; at worst they deflected minds from the search for real truths.

Malebranche extended his delight at devising definitions and rules for mental operations by postulating three rules of thumb that would launch one in the proper direction of exact thinking (besides the six rules for the systematic development of mental habits cited earlier). Once recognizing the general distinction between primary, quantitative truths and secondary, qualitative ones, the first rule was to determine the status of the question under examination, that is, whether or not one was seeking a relation of magnitude or one of quality. If the latter appeared to be the case, a second rule was needed: one must excise all equivocation from the terms of the question in order to give each term one meaning and one meaning only—in effect transforming the problem into one of quantitative relations.[48] Truths were to be univocal, and it is clear that Malebranche's desire for univocity was drawn from his understanding of numbers as the archetype of univocal truths. Each number could have only a single, consistent, even eternal meaning. One could never 'shade' into another meaning, say from one to two to three, as from red to red-orange to orange. Between one and two there is 1½ or 1¾ or an infinity of exact terms that are devoid of any equivocation, but not blends. Such blending rendered cognitions based on sensations inexact and fortuitous. Finally, having expunged equivocation from the terms of the question, one needed to consider the condition of the terms expressed in it. This meant to determine in a mathematical sense which remaining univocal terms were variable, which were constant, which were unknown, and what specific relations could be established between them.[49] This accomplished, one was in a stellar position to discover new and exact truths.

As Malebranche developed his theory of truths as relations, he made it clear that the most important meaning of relation was "magnitude." In fact in the sixth book of the *Recherche* he moved beyond his earlier position that magnitude was a type of relation to the declaration that magnitude was synonymous with relation itself: "But it is necessary to remark that all relations or all reasons, simple as well as compound, are true magnitudes, and that the term magnitude itself is a relative term that marks necessarily some relation."[50] There is a piece of illogical legerdemain in moving from the statement that all magnitudes are relations to the converse assertion that all relations are magnitudes. ('All *S* is *P*' does not convert logically to 'all *P* is *S*'.) But this was without doubt intentional on Malebranche's part, because he saw in magnitude the essential means for communicating genera and unifying sciences, since magnitude unified both number and extension[51] and as such was the object of both algebra and geometry. "All magnitude being therefore a relation, or all relation a magnitude, it is evident that one can express all relations by ciphers and represent them to the imagination by lines."[52] Only through number and extension could one know any relations at all: "These ideas are the clearest and most evident of all . . . [and] above all, one must apply one's reason to the ideas of numbers and extension . . . [to discern] the immutable rules and common measures of all other things that we know and that we are able to know."[53] One can scarcely overstress Malebranche's explicit recognition of the significance of magnitude as the object of mathematics, as synonymous with relations, and as the model for all reasoning with evidence. In his debate with Arnauld over the nature of ideas, he framed one of his most unambiguous statements concerning its central importance: "The object of pure mathematics is magnitude in general, which includes: 1. abstract numbers with their properties; 2. *intelligible extension* with all the lines and figures one can discover."[54] Descartes' dream had led him to affirm the communication of what had been conceived previously as the two distinct genera, arithmetic and geometry, from which he postulated the unity of all scientific knowledge. In conceiving magnitude as the conceptual foundation for the intuitions of both the "number-thing" and the "extension-thing" (to use Ortega's phrasing), Malebranche was making explicit Descartes' vision. While it is true that the Oratorian held in the first edition of the *Recherche* that the relations of extension were in a strict sense only sense perceptions—that magnitude was spatial—this position was ambiguous, as we shall see in the next chapter. In any case the communication of geometrical perceptions with numbers through the concept of magnitude implied that extension relations were reducible to the exact thinking of pure abstraction and that the essence of magnitude could no longer be purely spatial in its "thingness" but was purely relational.

After identifying relation with magnitude, Malebranche described the purely relational order of magnitude. Magnitude itself, as indicated in the passage cited above, was but "a relative term." There could be no term "large by itself" or existing without relation to some other term.[55] Numbers were simply relations, or ratios; four was the ratio of 4:1, or $^4/_1$, or otherwise expressed as the ratio of 8:2 or $^8/_2$. And in a ratio the meaning of any term depended solely and necessarily upon its position with respect to other terms.[56] Accordingly, all relations of magnitude were reducible to two: equality, which was the exact relation between two identical terms; and inequality, which required the intermediary of an "exact measure" in order to specify the comparative positions of unequal magnitudes. As a term that made possible the exact expression of all relations of inequality and thus reduced them to identity, the exact measure was "a simple idea and perfectly intelligible" in itself, "a universal measure" that could accommodate itself to all sorts of subjects.[57] The name Malebranche gave that term was *unité*, and it is with his concept of *unité* that we arrive at the center of his epistemological vision.

Malebranche's idea of *unité* has been discussed infrequently by scholars. This is understandable, if lamentable, because Malebranche himself did not dwell at any great length on the concept, although its significance was capital. One scholar who has noted its importance, André Robinet, has called attention to both the "prevalence" of the idea of *unité* in Malebranche's theory of mathematics as the cornerstone of magnitude and to its double meaning. Robinet discerns two senses of *unité*—the one metaphysical, marked by indivisibility; the other purely mathematical, an operational definition, marked by divisibility.[58] This interpretation is not without grounds. In the first edition of the *Recherche*, *unité* was defined as a necessary feature of magnitude and consequently as the foundation of number relations. All relations in the natural order are reduced to equality or inequality; inequality is defined as more or less; and all operations seeking to identify exactly the relations of more or less are based on the addition or subtraction of *unité* or parts of *unité*: "Thus it is only by the addition and subtraction of *l'unité* and of parts of *l'unité* (when one considers it divided) that one measures all magnitudes exactly and discovers all truths."[59] Because numbers are relations or ratios they are conceived as collections of *unités*: "And because all numbers are composed only of *l'unité*, it is already evident that without the ideas of numbers and the manner of comparing and measuring these ideas, that is to say, without arithmetic, it is impossible to advance in the knowledge of compound truths."[60] As the chief component or building block of all numbers, *unité* is indivisible, a characteristic that for Malebranche is both analytical and metaphysical.[61] Jean Prestet, Malebranche's protégé, was even more explicit about the indivisibility of *unité*: "If the idea of *l'unité* contains indivisibility, it follows that all that is one is indivisible. . . . For if it were divisible and had parts, the idea of multitude would be proper, and thus *l'unité* would not be *l'unité*."[62] There is a sense in which this conception of *unité* is quite correct in mathematics. One per se is by definition never divisible; and when one writes a fraction, such as ¼, this may be read as stating that one is simply one of four equal parts, that when added to itself four times yields four, and when not added yields only ¼ of four. One is not divided or broken up into smaller bits but is merely expressed as related to other collections of ones. "*L'unité* to which 4 relates is not expressed, but understood, because 4 is a relation in the same way that $^4/_1$ or $^8/_2$ is, since 4 is equal to $^4/_1$ or $^8/_2$."[63] As analytical, *unité* is thus that term by which all other number relations are examined, and accordingly it does not subject itself to any further analysis. It is metaphysical because it is "simple," perfectly "intelligible," exact, "universal"—indeed eternal—all characteristics of a reality that transcends any mutable conditions.[64]

A second sense of *unité* was derived from the operations of mathematics and was presented most clearly by Prestet in his *Éléments des mathématiques*. Besides the *unité* that was "simple, indivisible, and without composition of any parts,"[65] Prestet saw in mathematics a "false *unité*" that must be conceived as divisible: "we choose from among compared magnitudes some one which represents and receives the name of *l'unité*, and we conceive this *unité* as divisible."[66] Malebranche also had acknowledged the supposed divisibility of *unité* in referring to the "parts" of the concept,[67] and in the final edition of the *Recherche*, he added a passage in which he indicated explicitly that *unité* must be divisible to infinity.[68] Such a description of *unité* was necessary to perform mathematical operations. True, by definition, *unité* could not be divided, but it had to be so conceived since, in order to compare magnitudes, the division *of* one was as essential as the division *by* one; and false unity "allows the division of *l'unité* into numbers, as *l'unité* divides numbers."[69] Prestet and Malebranche meant by the division of one that the notion of infinite divisibility was a necessary condition of continuous magnitudes. For example, in dealing with continua, such as lines, certain segments could be represented by an exact number. But more often an operation or function was required to express exactly a segment. The hypotenuse of an isosceles right triangle was a line segment, but one that could only be expressed symbolically as $\sqrt{2}$, and such an expression could not be resolved into an undivided *unité* or collection of *unités*. In fact, Malebranche noted in the 1712 edition of the *Recherche* that the achievement of calculus was to make possible the exact expression of the infinite functions of variables and thereby to provide a precise means of expressing the continuity of geometrical figures.[70]

Robinet contends that Malebranche's theory of mathematics exhibited this dualism between metaphysical and functional *unité* from its inception and that the dualism remained unresolved: "Therefore, one can state that nothing philosophically elaborated leads from the idea of indivisible *unité* to the idea of divisible *unité*."[71] This interpretation is a needed corrective of the earlier argument of Léon Brunschvicg that, in seeking to absorb geometry into algebra,[72] Malebranche's philosophy of mathematics suffered an implicit dualism between extension (geometry) and number (algebra), which was never successfully clarified. It is evident that in the concept of magnitude Malebranche saw these realms united, that any dualism in his mathematical theory must be sought in the concept of magnitude itself and in its basis *unité*. But Robinet is only partially correct in his interpretation of the nature of this dualism. And following the clue of the 'number' model enables us to recognize that the dualism in *unité* can be resolved—and was so resolved implicitly in Malebranche's mind—by reference to the features of 'number'.

The key to the meaning of *unité* in this resolution is found in the implications of its purely epistemic function as a "common measure." For, analogous to Descartes' conception that the problems of geometry were problems of order and not measurement, Malebranche perceived that *unité* possessed an epistemic value superseding that of a measuring device, because it revealed in fact the "natural order" of the relations one was trying to discover. It is imperative to realize that mathematical order was constantly the focus of Malebranche's concern. To have a clear grasp of the "true order of things," "the order of nature," that is an "immutable" expression of God's law, was the goal of science.[73] Clear and distinct truths yielded knowledge of that order, and the concept of *unité* as the cornerstone of clear and distinct truths exhibited the two most fundamental features pervading it: discreteness and continuity.

The French term '*unité*' implies as much. In contrast to English, which carries a clear distinction between unity and unit, *unité* serves as both. When it denotes unit, the reference is to the discrete and disparate ideas of numbers, to number in its cardinal definition; in instances where unity is the proper reading, the reference is to the continuous and whole number realm—"perfect in totality" is Descartes' phrase[74]—to number in its ordinal definition. As a unit, the concept was necessary to express exactly all relations of inequality. All numbers, whole and fractional, all algebraic equations, and all functions of calculus assumed the unit as a discrete, simple, irreducible term relating all "parts of magnitude" that were composed of it. Numbers "contain *l'unité*, or a determined number of equal parts of *l'unité*."[75] And the functions of mathematics likewise were functions of a discrete segment of magnitude. To take the square root of a number is to presuppose a unit or collection of units that is the subject of the function. "In each species of magnitude, therefore, one singles out such a determinate part as desired, by means of *l'unité* or the common measure."[76] Further, discreteness is a necessary condition for the relation of equality, since mathematical equality is the exact, one-to-one correspondence between unit members of any two or more classes. The sense of indivisibility, then, which Malebranche contended lay at the basis of *unité* can be seen to connote clearly the cardinality of number.

If this is so, it is equally apparent that *unité* as divisible expressed for Malebranche the central notion of ordinality, continuity or repetition to infinity of any mental act. Malebranche revealed this intuition when he noted that *unité* did not stand alone as a measure or cornerstone but was to be regarded as a concept relative to infinity.[77] Here the conception is of a natural, mathematical order of increasing magnitude that is everywhere dense. Between terms an infinite number of other terms can be interpolated and any series of terms may be extrapolated infinitely. The properties of numbers were thus "infinitely infinite;" so too with geometrical continua, for example, the sides of a triangle may be lengthened or shortened to infinity.[78] Finally, the relation of inequality, characterized by more or less, reflected the mathematical continuum of increasing magnitude and its density. The dual sense of *unité*, its divisibility and indivisibility, therefore reveals in Malebranche the predominance of the two chief aspects of the idea of number: the cardinal and ordinal concepts. And the emphasis he placed on *unité* and magnitude as the basis of order in his theory of relations points to the single and unifying, indeed dominant, vision of 'number' as the guiding force in his conception of the nature of truths. This dominant vision enabled Malebranche to move away from his earlier emphasis on the discreteness (or indivisibility) of numbers in the first edition of the *Recherche* to embrace the continuity (or divisibility) of 'number' in the 1712 edition and also to accept fully the calculus of Leibniz and Newton.[79] Furthermore, the same dominant vision made possible the shift from considering ideas as discrete, in his first theory of the vision in God, to acknowledging the continuity of ideas as expressed in the theory of intelligible extension. Far from being an irreducible dualism, the two senses of *unité* reveal the thoroughness with which Malebranche's science of magnitude, the key to all other sciences, was imbued with the model of 'number'.

It is difficult to overemphasize the significance of 'number' in Malebranche's perception of science. The *Recherche* reads like a crescendo, albeit a tortuous one, that culminates in *unité* and is then followed by the rules for correct scientific reasoning which are based upon it. Once this is acknowledged, other pieces of the Malebranche puzzle begin to fall into place. One such piece, mentioned briefly earlier, is Malebranche's notion of "evidence." Evidence, he held, was intimately united with truth; it was in fact "the character of truth," and reasoning "by evidence" connoted grasping the truth clearly and distinctly. When this occurred the mind rested; at other times its natural state was inquietude.[80] Doubt thus could be resolved only through evidence, the "clear and distinct view of all the parts and relations of the object that are needed to sustain a sound judgment."[81] This was the scientist's realm; in seeking to discover necessary relations he would not lapse into the scholastic error of confusing "evidence, which results from the comparison of ideas," with the "liveliness of feelings" that served only to confuse and blind.[82] He would seek, rather, those univocal chains of deductions, beginning with the simplest relations, then leading to relations between those relations, and finally ad infinitum to increasingly complex truths: "Not only is there a relation between ideas, but also between relations that are between ideas, between relations of relations of ideas, and finally between collections of many relations and between relations of these collections of relations, and so on to infinity: that is to say, there are truths compounded to infinity."[83] We are reminded of Dantzig's description of number as the basis of mathematics. From numbers emerge arithmetical relations ("relations between ideas"); these are generalized into the formulae of algebra ("relations . . . between relations"); the functions of algebra are in turn generalized into expressions of calculus ("relations . . . between relations of these collections of relations"). Malebranche clearly saw in mathematics this progression toward greater abstraction and generality: "However, algebra and analysis are yet an entirely different thing from arithmetic; they divide the mind's capacity much less. . . . A particular arithmetic operation discovers only one truth; a similar algebraic operation discovers an infinity of them."[84] All knowledge involved such reasoning with evidence, which he oftentimes called "a *geometrical* reason, or simply a *reason*," reasoning that yielded the "necessary connection between all parts of our lengthiest deductions."[85]

In Malebranche's theory of truth as relational, then, it is evident that he envisioned a new order of cognitions, one diametrically opposed to the generic relations of subject and modification. It was an order determined by the evidence of clear and distinct truths, and this evidence revealed it to be mathematical: constituted by the relations greater than, less than, or equal to; expressing the natural order of increasing magnitude and the arithmetic continuum to infinity; restricted to the realm of pure conception and freed from the wiles of the senses —or any other extrasystemic reference. Science was not at all concerned with the essences and attributes of things; it ignored the question of what it is to be something. We have no means of knowing objectively the 'substance' of magnitudes, only the relationships of things and their parts. "Thus," writes Schrecker, "our scientific research can never attain anything other than knowledge of quantitative relations. . . . The ideal of our science is isomorphy with reality."[86] Scientific truth was to be patterned after the archetype herein described as 'number'.

CHAPTER 4

'Number': Ideas and Intelligible Extension

Malebranche's theory of truth as relational and the central concepts of magnitude and *unité* are not the only evidence for the prevalence of 'number' in his thought. In his discussion of ideas and intelligible extension, we find reflected key features of the cardinal and ordinal concepts and further substantiation of the extent to which he drew on mathematics for his theory of knowledge. For the present, bearing in mind the distinction between ontological and epistemological considerations, two questions emerge as central. What was Malebranche's conception of the epistemic nature of ideas and intelligible extension and of the order they presented to the mind in cognition? Second, how were ideas and intelligible extension related to nonideal reality?

There were at least three distinguishable manners in which Malebranche conceived of ideas. He himself admitted that his definition of the term "idea" and its use in the *Recherche* were equivocal.[1] Antoine Arnauld had criticised this equivocation of the term, noting that in the first two books of the *Recherche* it signified any modification of the mind, whereas in the third book ideas referred to "certain *beings representative* of objects, distinguished really from perceptions and objects."[2] Replying to Arnauld's criticism, Malebranche explained that the first sense was a general use of the term, whereas the second definition, more restricted and technical, was the proper meaning of idea. The claim that an idea is a representative being spawned a lengthy polemic between himself and Arnauld which terminated only with Arnauld's death (after which Malebranche was unable to resist a final, unanswerable sally). The nub of the disagreement was over the origin and nature of ideas. Basically Arnauld contended that, as representational, ideas were ontologically a factor of consciousness or mind itself, while Malebranche maintained their independent ontological existence as substances.[3] Despite the length and heat of the dispute, both stipulated that the epistemic function of an idea was to mediate objects existing in nature apart from the mind and to make them known to it. In short, the argument was over the being not the representational function of ideas. And because the dispute concerned the ontology of an idea, the focus centered on its generic description. Was an idea a substance of its own accord, or was it an attribute of the substance mind? Yet beyond the considerable effort and thought expended in seeking to justify ideas as substances (or even more generally as modifications of mind), a third meaning of idea emerged in Malebranche's writings, one that tended to obviate the generic description by considering ideas not as substances or attributes but as relations. This third sense of idea commands our attention. How did it come about and what did it signify?

In the first edition of the *Recherche* (1674) Malebranche drew a sharp distinction between ideas, which in the strict sense were representative beings, and truths, which were relations. Ideas were eternal and real and one saw them in God; truths were in effect neither real nor eternal since they could not be seen in God. Augustine, Malebranche said, had erred on this point: "Thus we do not say, as Saint Augustine says, that we see God in seeing truths, but in seeing the *ideas* of these truths: for the ideas are real, but the equality between ideas, which is truth, is not real."[4] One sees God in perceiving the ideas *of* truths not in perceiving the truths themselves. The function of ideas, in other words, was to represent to the knowing mind truths (or relations) that exist apart from it. These relations were not real, but the ideas representing them were and could be identified with God's substance. Ideas were the essences of things and as such could be given proper generic determination. The implication is that 'substance' served as a model for determining essences. But this was equivocal, even in the *Recherche*, for, as noted in the last chapter, Malebranche also defined truths as "real relations." How could relations be both real and not real? While deferring examination of Malebranche's concept of reality, it is instructive to note here how the concept functioned to bring ideas and relations into synonymy. This identification came about as he reflected further on St. Augustine, particularly on Augustine's contention that numbers, like ideas, were eternal and thus seen in God.[5] Numbers, Malebranche acknowledged, were real essences because they were composed of *unité* and *unité* was indivisible and essential. The "essences of things consist of the indivisible," and therefore "are similar to numbers."[6] But ideas were essences too. Numbers and ideas must therefore be equal to one another (things equal to the same thing are equal to each other). It followed that because numbers were also relations and relations were truths, ideas must be truths and must be seen as mathematical in the same sense as truths. The distinction between truths and the ideas that represented them collapsed, as he eventually recognized: "If therefore, abstract numbers, which St. Augustine calls divine and eternal, and which are the ideas by which we count numbered things, are not distinguished from the transitory perceptions of our mind, certainly the truths of numbers will not be eternal and immutable."[7] Thus truths and ideas, both of which are eternal and divine, were united through numbers, and the relational description given truths on the model of 'number' was extended to embrace the realm of ideas. Essence was in effect transformed into relation and was no longer purely generic.

Two other examples help illustrate this transformation. In the *Entretiens* (1687) Malebranche distinguished between two types of ideas, those that were clear and those possessing "falseness or obscurity."[8] The message of this passage is that when an idea is clear or true, it is a relation; when it is obscure or false it is not. The distinction thus rests on the designation of ideas as relations not as beings or modifications. Second, in the penultimate year of his life the identification of clear and distinct ideas with the relations of number and extension was brought into even sharper focus. To present a demonstration, he wrote, "is to develop a clear idea and to deduce with evidence what this idea necessarily includes. And, it seems to me, the only ideas we have clear enough to make these demonstrations are those of extension and numbers."[9] Clearly then the identification of idea with truth and relation lent a new meaning to idea which was independent of the matrix of the ontological dispute between Malebranche and Arnauld.

This third sense of ideas, it is equally clear, mirrored the same characteristics of 'number' as had the description of truths. True, Malebranche called ideas essences that are immutable and eternal. But even as he used the language of 'substance', his meaning was drawn from 'number'. Not only were ideas identical to truths, their "essentiality" lay in their discreteness. And such discreteness was not the generic, particular term elicited from an undifferentiated field of sensation in the manner of the schoolmen but the discreteness of *unité*, reflecting the cardinal concept. Likewise the immutability and infinity of ideas hinged on continuity and the ordinal concept. Thus Malebranche wrote of ideas as infinite in an extrapolative sense, as with the idea of extension, which is infinite "because we are certain that we do not know how to exhaust it or find the end of it."[10] We could never conceive a limit to the act of counting, the consequence of which implied "an infinity of intelligible *unités*."[11] Also, between any two ideas there always existed another idea, ad infinitum—infinity in its interpolative sense. The order of truths as relations between ideas was equally an order of ideas that were themselves relations—in the same way that relations between numbers were in effect relations between relations "compounded to infinity."

This was the relational order that the mind received in cognition. Because truths and ideas were eternal and unchanging, Malebranche considered the process of acquiring them to be purely passive from the standpoint of the knowing mind. The mind never created truths ex nihilo but simply discovered them; never brought them forth from its own spontaneity but received them from without.[12] There were two kinds of reception of which the mind was capable: it could receive sensory information or "sensible" perceptions as he termed them in the *Recherche*; second, it could receive purely conceptual ideas, or "pure perceptions."[13] Following the Cartesian tradition, inasmuch as sensible perceptions were modifications of the mind itself, only in receiving pure perceptions did one grasp objective truths whose objectivity transcended the particular knowing mind. The most basic of these pure perceptions was "a simple thing," an example of which occurred "when one perceives two times 2 or 4."[14] In other words, simple perceptions were relations, and this is why Malebranche later called them ideas. Whereas Descartes had utilized the notion of "simple essences" in a mathematical manner to refer to the ratios or relations that dominated a series of deductions, Malebranche made "simple perceptions" the explicit basis of conceptual order. From simple perceptions larger reasonings are constructed. As Schrecker indicates the simple relations are not subject to further analysis; they serve as the components for all other truths and accordingly correspond "to our notion of axioms, which characterise extension and numbers and serve as the base of all mathematics."[15] For Malebranche the understanding receives these simple perceptions or mathematical relations. Judgment enters the cognitive process when the perception involves a comparison of two or more simple relations, such as $2 \times 2 = 4$, $2 \times 2 < 5$, and $2 \times 2 > 3$. To judge is to perceive a relation of equality or inequality, the latter constituted of the exact relations greater or smaller. The distinction between a judgment and a simple perception is somewhat artificial because the relations of equal, greater, or smaller are implicit in any ratio and thus in any number. Malebranche's point here was not that a judgment differs qualitatively from a simple perception but that the mental objects received are more complex. Comparisons of two or more judgments constituted a reasoning. To illustrate, Malebranche wrote that a reasoning unites the judgments $2 \times 2 = 4$ and $4 < 6$ in the expression $2 \times 2 < 6$. Although schematically one could detect a difference between a simple perception, a judgment, and a reasoning according to the complexity of the ideas or relations received, there was in fact "no other difference on the part of the understanding between a simple perception, a judgment, and a reasoning."[16] The function of the "pure understanding" was to receive the idea relations that constituted the order of truths.

To sum up thus far, for Malebranche we possess truths with certainty when we receive pure ideas. Ideas themselves are relational, vis-à-vis generic, and the relations we receive are those of magnitude, comprised of greater than, less than, and equal to. Magnitude is the object of all mathematics and combines the intuitions of number and extension. The cornerstone of magnitude is *unité*, and *unité* is doubly ambiguous: metaphysically it is both indivisible and infinitely divisible; epistemically it is both discrete and continuous. Thus when we perceive an object or body "scientifically," we know the mathematical relationships between the parts of the body itself, that is, its "configuration," and its mathematical relations to other bodies in geometrical space.[17]

The theory of intelligible extension was Malebranche's most mature formulation of the above conception. This theory was introduced in "Éclaircissement X" to the *Recherche* in order to amplify and clarify the notion that we see all things in God. The clarification was needed to counter criticism put forth by Simon Foucher, who charged Malebranche with having maintained in the *Recherche* that particular, material objects were seen in God, rendering Him in some sense particular and material.[18] Intelligible extension therefore was designed to account for both particularity and universality in a manner that would not limit God in any fashion. The conclusion that God contains all ideas (the vision *in* God) was formulated by Malebranche in the *Recherche* after examining and refuting four alternative explanations for the origins of ideas.[19] Because ideas are in God, they must be infinite; because they are infinite, God contained them before the creation of the universe and before the creation of any particular bodies. God had in himself an infinity of possible worlds and contained the ideas of material substances but without becoming material himself.[20] His word was the idea of all that is and of all that possibly could be. This idea was divisible and composed of parts in the same way that all created bodies, material extension, were constituted of relations of distance.[21] As the parts of material extension could be divided according to the various configurations comprising the material objects of nature, so too could the ideas of intelligible extension be analysed into various configurations, relations, and figures without in any manner limiting the substance of God. "This [intelligible] extension, having parts, can be divided in the same sense that it is extended, that is to say, into intelligible parts."[22] It is thus only the intelligible and not the material that God actually possesses or contains: "There is nothing in God that is figured really and in that way capable of movement, but there are in God intelligible figures, and, as a consequence, intelligible movements."[23]

Intelligible extension then affirms the identification of conceptual truths, but not material reality, with the word and wisdom of God; it is the entire relational realm of ideas and truths, the archetype of the material world that we inhabit and the archetype of an infinity of other possible worlds.[24] This archetype of ideas and truths is, to repeat, no hierarchy wherein terms coalesce into categories of increasingly greater abstraction and generality; segments of intelligible extension, like those of material extension, are all of equal value, and because "the parts of intelligible extension are all of the same nature, they can all represent whatever bodies there may be."[25] All intelligible ideas represent potential bodies; that they represent actual bodies depends entirely on the will of God which has brought a particular body into actuality.[26] Each idea or relation is thus universal in its own right because it participates in the infinity of the universal order that makes up intelligible extension. Each relation derives its meaning solely from its relation to other ideas which are of equal and univocal value. For example, $(3)^2+(4)^2=(5)^2$ describes a particular circle whose radius is the hypotenuse of a right triangle with sides of three and four units. The "definition" of the triangle (and thus the circle) is presented completely in the exact relationships of its sides. The triangle is both particular, inasmuch as its sides are composed of particular line segments designated by numbers, and general, because it fulfills the relation or formula

$a^2+b^2=c^2$, as every right triangle and every circle must. The formula's generality or universality means that its relations hold for an infinity of possible particular relations, that is, any circle with a diameter of 2, 3, 4, . . . n units.[27] In this way "the mind joins to its finite ideas, without reflection, the idea of generality it finds in the infinite."[28] Seeing things in God or by means of His intelligible extension is seeing them, in Schrecker's words, "*sub specie mathematica*, as constituted by the intelligible relations . . . of magnitude; we see in God the quantitative order of things, and not their essence."[29]

What then of the relation between intelligible and material extensions? To answer this question we need to recognize an equivocation that traverses Malebranche's writings on extension. Léon Brunschvicg has been instrumental in identifying this equivocation. On the one hand, he notes, Malebranche conceived of two distinct extensions: "But you ought to distinguish two species of extension, the one intelligible, the other material."[30] Yet, on the other hand, Malebranche explicitly denied two extensions, maintaining that one was sufficient: "No, Ariste, there are not two kinds of extension, nor two kinds of ideas that represent them."[31] How is this apparent contradiction to be understood? Brunschvicg's interpretation derives from his contention, mentioned earlier, that Malebranche reduced physics to geometry and geometry to algebra and that intelligible extension is a purely algebraic notion. Malebranche, he argues, translated geometric quality (the intuition of space) and with it material extension into algebraic quantity (the intuition of number), and consequently Malebranche spiritualized or intellectualized material extension completely.[32] Jean Laporte offers an opposing view. He cites Malebranche's insistence upon identifying intelligible extension, the archetypal idea of the created universe, with God's substance insofar as it is representative of material bodies, as evidence that intelligible extension must remain totally distinct from material extension, God's creation. The distinction must be maintained, claims Laporte, because of the clear division between a body that is extended and has length, depth, and width and the idea of a body that represents it, an idea that is not extended in length, depth, and width. The separation of the two extensions is a result of the Cartesian dualism of mind and matter.[33] While Brunschvicg's interpretation unites the two extensions epistemologically, Laporte's reading maintains their ontological disjunction. Both of these interpretations can be supported from Malebranche's writings and both are partially correct. But a deeper understanding emerges with the recognition that each of them accords with the pattern of 'number' and can thus be explained through reference to this basic vision.

To show how we must focus first on intelligibility rather than on extension per se. Here Brunschvicg's reading, though partially correct, suffers the defect of identifying the realm of intelligible extension too closely *with* algebra. Instead a more correct reading, as Dominick Iorio has noted in his valuable dissertation on intelligible extension, shows that in Malebranche's conception "algebra is itself subordinate to intelligible extension and reduced to it."[34] The order of ideas was structurally identical to the order of space and therefore to all material bodies. This order functioned in two spheres: the ideal, the order of abstract numbers and algebraic relations; and the material, the order of counted things and geometrical relations.[35] Responding to the third letter of Arnauld, Malebranche argued that only through knowledge of abstract numbers could we count things or grasp the relations that bodies assumed in their various configurations. All knowledge presupposed this intelligibility: "It is by these *divine and immutable* numbers, present to all intelligent beings, that arithmeticians augment their learning, and merchants keep their accounts."[36] Only by using abstract number and the relations of algebra could one express intelligibly the figures embodying the proper objects of geometry. Because geometrical figures could be known properly only through abstract relations, they must be considered like number, eternal and immutable. Malebranche then cited a long passage from St. Augustine in support of this thesis and concluded with this telling remark: "It is clear from these passages of St. Augustine, and from a hundred others one will find in his books, that intelligible extension, and the geometers' figures that cannot be conceived without this extension, are eternal and immutable; that they [figures] can be perceived only in the sovereign truth that includes them; and that one must be blind not to see this."[37] Intelligible extension, which we might more appropriately call ideal extension, and geometry figure equally in the same truth, which is intelligibility itself, sovereign reason, the word of God.

Intelligibility, then, is God's substance insofar as it is participated in by material bodies and grasped through ideas by the knowing mind. It is not dependent in any manner upon material bodies or the mind for its meaning. Intelligibility is meaning. And the relations that constitute it require no extra-systemic connection for their grounding. This is not merely a subsumption of geometry into algebra, or the algebraicization of material extension, as Brunschvicg contends, but of both geometry and algebra—both extensions—into a vision of 'number', for it is the nature of intelligibility to reflect those relations that we have characterized by 'number'.[38] This is why Malebranche insisted on the "archetypal" character of the Divine Word or Universal Reason, which "includes in its substance the primordial ideas of all beings, created and possible."[39] When we contemplate intelligible extension, we see "the archetype of the material world we inhabit, and that of an infinity of other possible worlds." Not only is there an infinity of possible worlds but an infinity unbounded in any fashion: "Thus there is only God, only the infinite, only undetermined being, or only the infinitely infinite infinite that can contain infinitely infinite reality."[40] A vision of 'number' provides the order of intelligibility for Malebranche. Knowledge requires subsuming any objects into this order, be those objects ideal, as with numbers or algebraic relations (which embrace all possible worlds), or material, as with the figures and bodies of our actual world. Intelligibility therefore functioned in Malebranche's theory of the vision in God, and later in the theory of intelligible extension, to unite ideal extension and material extension, just as magnitude had united arithmetic (or algebra) and geometry.

We have argued to this point that epistemically both types of extension, intelligible (or ideal) and material, were united by their structure, intelligibility itself, which reflected the model of 'number'. Malebranche expressed the unification of these orders with several phrases. He often spoke of intelligible extension as "representing" bodies, as comprising the divine substance insofar as it is related to bodies, or as it is "participated in" by them. All three phrases can even be found in a single passage: "But you do not see it [divine substance] in itself, or according to what it is. You see it only according to the relation it has to material creatures, only insofar as it is participated in by them, or only as it is representative of them."[41] The phrases "participated in" and "representative of" are repeated frequently throughout Malebranche's writings to express the relation between extension or matter and God's substance, intelligibility, which man can understand to a limited measure.[42] That these phrases are pivotal is beyond doubt. Not only are they repeated frequently, but they are employed in key passages. They need to be properly understood and to do so requires examination of the concept of "representing."

In scholastic usage "representing" implied a metaphysical or essential likeness between an object and that which represented, or re-presented, it. On this theory, there must be an essential likeness between an object in nature and the idea that represented it mediately to the knowing mind.[43] This likeness was similar to the essential likeness between cause and effect. An effect must contain as much reality as the cause but not more; hence the cause must be like it with respect to that reality. Aquinas expressed this idea when he wrote that effects "pre-exist in a cause according to its mode of being."[44] Resemblance between cause and effect, and between object and representation, implied sharing a common form that was at once an epistemic and an ontological notion.[45] Through form in knowledge a correspondence was established between the "object-as-known" and the "object-in-itself." This correspondence was not merely a copy in the sense that an idea provided the image of the object but was described technically as the "adequation" of the "thing-as-known" to the "thing-in-itself." Again, Aquinas:

> But all knowledge is perfected by the assimilation of the knower to the thing known, so that that assimilation is said to be the cause of the knowledge. . . . Consequently, the first comparison of the thing which is to understanding is that the thing which is correspond to the understanding, which correspondence is called the adequation of the thing and the understanding. . . . It is this, consequently, which the true adds over and above that which is: namely conformity or adequation of the thing and understanding, and to this conformity as has been said, the knowledge of the thing follows.[46]

Aquinas went on to outline how the process of adequation was developed through the senses and, in so doing, generally reflected the pattern of thinking described here as 'substance'. Implicit in the scholastic definition of adequation or correspondence was the assumption that the object in the world of sensory experience imposed some cognitive structure upon the ideas that represented it, that there was a causal connection between the object and the idea. This theory was still prominent in the seventeenth century.[47] One of the most penetrating critics of Cartesianism, Simon Foucher, resorted to it frequently, claiming that no sense could be made of a representation that did not possess an essential likeness to the object represented. Moreover, if ideas were to represent objects in the material world (as the Cartesians held), they must be in a metaphysical sense "like" the material world and hence the radical ontological distinction between mind and matter would fall.[48]

Malebranche was quite aware of this problem, particularly as he was the target for some of Foucher's most incisive criticism. He plainly intended to develop the notion of representation, participation, or correspondence along different lines than those held by the canon of Dijon. The outlines of his theory were grounded in the concept of mathematical correspondence connoted by the cardinal idea of number, a one-to-one relation between members of different classes. Again Malebranche did not consciously identify cardinality as the basis of his conception, but evidence abounds that he sought a new description of correspondence and that his new description reflected his mathematical instincts.

This new meaning of correspondence marked something of a departure from Descartes, although as indicated in Chapter 2 the suggestion of mathematical correspondence can be found in his writings. Descartes, we also recall, had uneasily maintained the substantial unity of soul and body, his more famous distinction between the two notwithstanding.[49] Malebranche openly denied this unity; soul and body, he held, could be joined only by means of a mutual correspondence between the modifications of soul and those of body.[50] One of his earliest expressions of this correspondence is found in the first edition of the *Recherche*, where he made explicit the relation between thoughts, which, properly speaking, belong to the soul, and brain traces that were the end product of a mechanistic process of sensation: "All union of mind and body that is known to us consists of a natural and mutual correspondence of thoughts of the soul with traces of the brain, and of emotions of the soul with movements of animal spirits."[51] There could be no necessary connection between soul and body, according to Malebranche, in the sense that modifications of the body caused or shared an essential likeness with thoughts or vice versa. "There is no necessary connection between the presence of an idea in a man's mind and the existence of the thing that this idea represents."[52] The relation between the two was purely extrinsic. How then did we have guarantees that our ideas represented or corresponded to matter at all? His full answer is found in the doctrine of occasionalism, of which more later, but in the *Recherche* he sketched three criteria for establishing the relation between ideas and brain traces. The first of these was "nature, or the constant and immutable will of the Creator."[53] It was simply a law of nature, established by the continually creative will of God, that, when we receive an imprint in our brain, we receive on the same occasion an idea in our mind (here idea means any object of thought or modification of mind—volition, sensation, imagination, pure idea), an idea that corresponds to the imprint. "The union of the soul with the body consists of the mutual correspondence of movements of the one with thoughts of the other, since such a correspondence is sufficient to explain all that passes between them."[54] For example, when the light carrying the image of a tree strikes the eye, it activates the mechanism of vision, which in turn carries the light to the brain, where a corresponding idea occurs, in this case a sensation, in the mind. This sensation idea is not something elicited from the physical experience like the mental extracts of traditional thought but is something entirely outside the bodily processes to which an impulse in the mechanism of sensation corresponds.

The second criterion for the correspondence, Malebranche claimed, was "the identity of the time" of traces and ideas; the correspondence must be concurrent. Having once been received, ideas could then be held in the memory and recalled at a later time, but their initial reception neither preceded nor followed the motions of the "animal spirits" in the order of time or in any causal manner. The third mark of the relation between traces and ideas is found in the will of men. As a man wills x, x occurs in the brain traces and a bodily motion results. This occurs not because of any causal connection between the volition and the consequence but because of a correspondence between them in accordance with the more general laws of motion established by God. Thus God has established for man's conservation that, when man wills to act, his willing (a purely mental modification) is accompanied by his acting (a modification of the body).[55]

This correspondence between ideas and traces, which underscored the correspondence between the intelligible and the material worlds, was not simply a case of the former being a copy of the latter, although the examples Malebranche used at times (and those cited above) appeared to so indicate. Despite these examples he insisted that no copying was involved: "One must not imagine that the intelligible world has such a relation with the material and sensible world that there is, for example, an intelligible sun, horse, and tree destined to represent to us the sun, a horse, and a tree."[56] If correspondence did not refer to copy and also excluded any intrinsic connection or essential likeness, of what did it consist? What did Malebranche mean when he spoke of bodies represented in intelligible extension? A passage from the *Entretiens* reveals a clue: "Intelligible extension, for example, represents bodies; it is their archetype or their idea. But although this extension occupies no place, bodies are, and can only be, locally extended. . . . Thus intelligible extension represents infinite spaces, but fills none of them, and although, to speak in the same manner, it fills all minds and makes itself known to them, it does not at all follow that our mind is spacious."[57] Intelligible extension occupies no space but is infinite; all bodies occupy space and are finite. Accordingly, when intelligible extension "represents" locally extended bodies, it neither becomes spatial nor do the bodies become infinite. But both extensions share the relations (or intelligibility) of which each is composed. That is, the relations constituting locally extended bodies (and, recall, all material extension is reduced to relations of distance) have a one-to-one correspondence with the purely conceptual and infinite relations of intelligible extension. Léon Brunschvicg, in citing this passage, states the relationship succinctly: "The relation of intelligible extension to extended bodies is exactly the relation of *abstract numbers* to *numbered things*."[58] The parts of intelligible extension, which are all of the "same nature" represent, or correspond to, any body whatsoever, just as abstract numbers can correspond to any numbered objects.[59] Whether there are six apples or six oranges has no direct bearing on the intelligibility of six; likewise with geometrical configurations: $a^2+b^2=c^2$ will be true regardless of whether we find a body that is actually circular. In fact, only by assuming the corresponding relation between any body and abstract idea, or archetype, can any body be known as circular, just as only perforce of the correspondence between abstract numbers and things can any thing be counted.[60]

This conception gained even clearer expression in some of Malebranche's last correspondence, that with Dortous de Mairan, in which he was seeking to make clear his own divergence from Spinoza. There he spoke continually of the relation of the "*idea suo ideato*,"[61] claiming that Spinoza had confused the infinity and necessity of the *idea* with the finitude and contingency of the *ideatum*: "The idea of extension is infinite, but its *ideatum* may not be. Perhaps there is actually not even any *ideatum* . . . and I am convinced that the idea has existed an eternity without the *ideatum*."[62] The relation between *idea* and *ideatum* may best be translated as the relation between the abstract idea and the 'idea-ed' thing, analogous to the relation between the abstract number and the numbered thing. That relation can only be a direct one-to-one correspondence. There is clearly no reference to any essential similarity of substances; the substances of mind and body remain distinct, as Laporte has argued. Indeed, according to Malebranche, Spinoza's error lay in confusing these egregiously. Also there is no copy of object by idea in the sense that the idea is simply an image that reproduces the object in some type of mental picture. The archetypal idea is utterly devoid of imagery, being essentially composed of pure relations and accessible to the mind solely through pure perceptions. Again Iorio's comments are suggestive:

> To say that experiences correspond to or are related to ideas is not to claim that experiences 'picture' in a concrete way some sort of mental 'picture'. Rather, what is meant here is that in some way the physical line and the sensible experience of a physical circle, plane, or triangle participate in or are isomorphically related to intelligible extension. Hence correspondence does not mean resemblance in this case any more than resemblance is meant when we say that the world corresponds to God's wisdom, or that the circle drawn on paper resembles the algebraic equation which expresses circularity or the geometric definition that one gives of a circle.[63]

Iorio is correct as far as he goes, but we need to take the next step and firmly identify the correspondence that unites mind and matter for Malebranche as the cardinal concept of number. It is just such a notion that traverses Malebranche's thought and enters at the key points: a one-to-one correspondence between brain traces and ideas; between abstract number and numbered thing; between *idea* and *ideatum*; between type and archetype. The Gordian knot of ontological adequation is severed with the cardinal concept.

Pursuing this a bit further enables clarification of another ambiguity already presented in this chapter but not resolved. We have seen that according to Brunschvicg intelligible extension for Malebranche was algebraicized and distinguished accordingly from geometry, which was simply the highest form of material extension, and perceived by the senses through seeing lined figures. This was Malebranche's position in the *Recherche*, where he maintained the primacy of algebra over geometry. Yet later on in the *Entretiens* he expressed clearly the proposition that geometry was included within the sphere of intelligible extension, that it was perfectly intelligible in its own right.[64] The ambiguity then is the position of geometry: did it belong properly to intelligible or to material extension? The answer is that it belonged to both through correspondence. It was considered part of material extension when the reference was to a correspondence between perceivable planes, lines, conic sections, and other geometrical figures and particular bodies in nature. The figure of an ellipse described the path of a planet, but it was also viewed as abstracted from a particular planet's orbit and was thus standing apart from, but corresponding to, the particular piece of extension it described. Composed of a curved line that was perceived, it remained in the realm of the materially extended. But what was a line? Having no depth or breadth by definition, it could not be locally extended and had to be considered as belonging to intelligible extension. Malebranche often used the phrase "circle in general," which was defined by its formula, to describe the ideal circularity of intelligible extension that corresponded to locally extended circles —either those drawn on paper or perceived imperfectly in nature. Bodies, in short, corresponded to geometrical figures, and geometrical figures corresponded to the ideal relations of intelligible extension. Geometry was thus at times given a meaner status than arithmetic and algebra, as in the *Recherche* where it is plain that Malebranche had in mind the established science of geometry and its use of compass and ruler in dealing with such problems as the trisection of an angle. But geometry was also of equal status with algebra when spatial magnitudes corresponded with number. The one-to-one correspondence between points and numbers, between intelligible *unités* and figures constructed from lines and points, meant that the exactitude of algebraic formulae was equally the exactitude of geometry. In sum, number and extension, algebra and geometry were united through intelligibility or magnitude, united by 'number'.

A final point of corroboration is in order. Malebranche often wrote of the distinction between "conceiving" or "perceiving" and "comprehending" when describing the function of the mind in knowledge. Although, as Schrecker has written, he was not always consistent in his employment of this distinction, he generally used it to refer to the difference between the manner in which we grasp mathematical infinity and the way we understand finite relations. Comprehending referred to the discerning and apprehension of a relation of which we have immediate, evident, and complete intellection, whereas conceiving or perceiving referred to complex relationships that followed necessarily by an uninterrupted progression from relations simply and immediately comprehended.[65] The truth of a relation did not depend upon its comprehensibility but on its conceivability.[66] For instance, to our comprehension infinity could only be without bounds, such that once we had removed all limits (for example, by claiming matter to be infinitely divisible), we had reached the end of comprehension. It made no sense to speak of an 'infinity plus one' or to compare infinities. (We count to infinity, theoretically, and therefore we shall reach a last number at the infinite end of our series. But all numbers are either odd or even, hence infinity must be odd or even, a nonsensical statement.) Yet such comparisons were made repeatedly in mathematics as with comparisons of the incommensurables.[67] The only way in which we could grasp these comparisons was through conception not through comprehension. So, likewise, with imaginary numbers. They could be conceived but not comprehended. (We comprehend number as magnitude; magnitude is positive, composed of *unités*; negative numbers express negative magnitudes, a sensible enough notion. But taking the square root of a negative number, such as -1, puts us into the realm of nonsense if we are left solely to our comprehension, for we must seek a magnitude, negative or positive, which when multiplied by itself will result in a negative magnitude, a logical impossibility since a magnitude multiplied by itself is always positive.) Hence we cannot comprehend imaginaries, although we can conceive them because of the relations and functions that constitute mathematical operations. Truth is in the realm of conceivability or perceivability not comprehension: "For it is established that the mind perceives the infinite, although it does not comprehend it."[68] The truth of a relation or an idea depends not on its comprehensibility, which is only a quality of the mind, but solely on conceivability—its position relative to other relations. We could even conceive a solid of more than three dimensions, although we could never comprehend it.[69] The purpose of this distinction is thus to facilitate the assimilation of mathematical truths, those pure idea relations that constitute knowledge.

In the Middle Ages it was commonplace to distinguish between *scientia* and *sapientia*, the former referring to knowledge of nature, science, the latter referring to knowledge of things pertaining to God, providence, or wisdom.[70] Ideas, we recall, were part of God's wisdom. In employing the term idea to designate the contents of human thought, Descartes was instrumental in univocalising knowledge, thus making *scientia* and *sapientia* part and parcel of the same order and in expanding man's knowledge by uniting science and mathematics. It is evident that Malebranche continued this evolution. In his epistemology and conception of science he focused, like Descartes, on the model or archetype of 'number' as his guide. But things pertaining to science were, for the Oratorian, equally things pertaining to God, and thus both were brought into the same realm. Our ideas were God's and vice versa, at least insofar as we could conceive them. God's order and man's were identical, and that order, as we have seen, was one of univocal truths, infinite in its extension and composed of an infinity of intelligible parts, each of which was a relation. To engage in science for Malebranche meant to understand this order of truths as much as humanly possible—to become a "savant." It was no longer an effort to classify the objects of the natural world nor to grasp their generic essences. It was rather to see intelligibility as mathematical and, once grasping this intelligibility, to realize that it expressed the possible order of all existents. The meaning of the terms of intelligible extension was in no regard dependent upon those existents but solely upon position, the relation to *unité* and to other numbers, just as the meaning of ideas in God's mind, for scholastics, did not depend on any relation to existents in the world. The abstractions of algebra, and ultimately calculus, were all infinite, for they were founded upon the principle of mathematical induction, the assumption that we can always pass from a number to its successor, that the act of counting may be repeated an infinite number of times. The order of truths, in sum, was the order that we have described with the ordinal concept of number. And the connection of that order to experience of the natural world was a connection of correspondence. It was the correspondence of the relations perceived in material extension to those of intelligibility itself, and, as has been argued, such correspondence was grounded in the cardinal concept of number. A new order for experience and a new connection between that order and experience—such was the science founded on 'number'.

CHAPTER 5

The Pattern of 'Substance'

The extent to which 'number' as a submerged model of thought provided the cohesion for Malebranche's understanding of science is by now evident—evident but incomplete. In fact, Malebranche's principal preoccupation was not really science, at least in the sense of wresting secrets from nature with a scientific method. He studied mathematics and Cartesian physics as preparation for writing the *Recherche* but after its publication paid little further heed to scientific and even to mathematical developments for the next fifteen years (1675–90).[1] During this period theological writings and the numerous polemical disputes precipitated by critical reaction to the *Recherche* commanded his attention. About 1690 his interest in science revived and was to remain animate for the rest of his life. His contributions to the dissemination of Leibnizian and Newtonian calculi date from these decades,[2] and his achievements in this regard were acknowledged by an invitation to join the Académie des Sciences in 1699.[3] Yet even then he remained more the student and observer of science than one of its practitioners, never abandoning his theology and polemics, and he continually subordinated his interest in science to an Oratorian vocation that centered on the philosophical and theological examination of the truths of Christianity.[4] Throughout his life Malebranche's concern for science always revolved around the principal question of how scientific knowledge and scientific discoveries accorded with truths of the Christian faith. Descartes had left these problems to theologians, while preserving the province of science and epistemology as his own. In accepting Cartesianism, Malebranche, to the contrary, was challenged to elucidate the new order of learning in language and terms consistent with religious truths, and in a fashion that could give the latter new illumination.[5] He was to be to Descartes what Aquinas had been to Aristotle.

But the era of the *Summae* was finished. In its stead was the profound intellectual tension of the seventeenth century which dwelt in Malebranche's thought. This was not merely the issue of contradictory statements, of which there were many.[6] As we have seen, apparent contradictions frequently can be resolved by appeal to a more basic vision, as for example with the resolution of the dual senses of *unité* and extension by reference to 'number'. The tension in Malebranche's thought lay deeper. It was a tension between visions, between ages even, that pervaded his work. While his science was founded firmly upon 'number', his metaphysics and theology, and with them the backbone of his religious discourse, were formulated along the model of 'substance'. This model was altered in Malebranche's conception and in some ways quite radically from scholastic expression. Yet it clearly retained much of its intellectual vigor. The purpose of the next two chapters is to demonstrate its presence and significance, first by examining Malebranche's adherence, ambiguous though it was, to the traditional language and pattern of 'substance', and second (in Chapter 6) by exploring some of the assumptions of 'substance' that Malebranche less ambiguously insisted on keeping.

A prima facie case for the persistence of 'substance' may initially be noticed in both the form and the content of the *Recherche*. The full title of the work reveals Malebranche's intention: *De la Recherche de la vérité: Où l'on traite de la nature de l'esprit de l'homme et de l'usage qu'il en doit faire pour éviter l'erreur dans les sciences.*[7] His goal explicitly stated here was to describe the "nature" of the mind, and this was in response to the implicit question: "What is it to be a mind?" Only from a description of what the mind is could he then move to a description of how the mind functions and subsequently devise a method that could assist it in avoiding error. Moreover, to achieve this end Malebranche resorted to a schematic outline reflective of the generic categorization of phenomena into classes. Following Descartes, he stipulated two classes of created substances: matter and mind. These two classes were similar in structure and could be compared generically with one another. The genus matter was divided into two species, figure and motion. The former referred to matter in its passive state; the latter defined matter in its activity. Likewise, mind was modified into two broad classifications, one passive, the understanding, and one active, the will. The passive-active distinction was qualified in both instances, for neither the will nor motion was truly active in the strict sense that either generated its own proper movement. To claim that the will was active meant strictly that it had the faculty of receiving many inclinations. So too with matter—its active state meant simply that it had the faculty of receiving motion.

This comparative hierarchy of substances continued. In the category of passive material states, that is, figure in general, there were two subspecies: figure narrowly speaking, which designated the shape of a body relative to other, external bodies; configuration, which referred to the "internal" relation of the parts of the body itself. Similarly, in the class of passive mental states (the understanding in general), there were two subspecies of mental passivity. Because the entire function of the understanding was to perceive ideas (here defined loosely as any object of perception) and because perception meant "receiving" ideas, the modification of the understanding was contingent upon the type of ideas it received. Ideas referred to objects either outside the mind, in which case the mental modification was sensation, or within it, in which instance the modification was properly termed imagination. (Malebranche further noted that, when the mind received ideas referring to objects outside the mind, such ideas were subdivided into two types: sensible perceptions, which were the mind's modifications; and pure perceptions, which he later defined as ideas in the strict sense. The latter, though united intimately to the mind by a "natural union," were not modifications of it but were part of the divine substance, of which more later.)[8]

This schematic description of mind and matter, which Malebranche outlined in the first chapter of the first book of the *Recherche*, provided the organizational structure for the entire work. Since the "nature" of the mind was so generically constituted in its modifications, it was reasonable to examine the mind attribute by attribute in order to describe it in detail and analyse the ways in which it errs. Accordingly, the first three books dealt with errors of the senses, imagination, and pure understanding, which collectively comprised the understanding in general or mind in its passive state. These were followed in turn by one book on the inclinations and one on the passions, both being attributes of mind in its activity. Only then was he ready to formulate and express his rules of method.

From this prima facie description of 'substance' arises the question of whether Malebranche viewed it as heuristic or as an accurate account of the mind's substantial reality. The question strikes at the heart of the historical nature of Cartesianism and invites more general formulation. Was the use of scholastic language and terminology merely an adventitious practice for Descartes, Malebranche, and others, occurring because such terminology comprised the language of philosophical discourse in the seventeenth century? Or was its use necessary and intentional, issuing from a desire to preserve basic meanings that such a language had expressed? As we saw earlier, Descartes' thought was somewhere between the two, neither wholly 'modern' nor bound totally by the trappings of scholasticism. In the case of Malebranche, even as he sought in the available language of substance philosophy to transform 'substance'—for example, to transform essence into relation—he also clearly intended to preserve central elements of the traditional pattern. The result was a twofold tendency: toward a substantiation of 'number' and toward a mathematization of 'substance'. The ambiguities in his treatment of the pattern of 'substance' may be best understood as features of this dual process.

With the proposition that all objects must be reduced to either being or a manner of being,[9] a claim he never wearied of repeating, Malebranche asserted that the language of 'substance' was not merely adventitious but necessary and essential to both science and metaphysics.[10] Desmond Connell has remarked that "implicit in his whole treatment [of ideas] is his conviction that all that exists is either a substance or a modification."[11] Nonetheless, there were clearly some departures from scholastic usage in his employment of these terms. Despite the hierarchy of genus and species in the *Recherche*, Malebranche firmly maintained that modifications of matter could not be qualitatively classified into distinct species. Rather, these modifications were simply different measures of distances: differences of degree not kind. Similarly, regarding mental attributes, Malebranche specified the differences between sense and imagination as ones of degree, "of more and less," not of quality or kind.[12] True, there was a crucial distinction between pure perceptions and sensible perceptions, but this was a difference between two separate substances—one created, the other uncreated—and not a division of classes subsumed under the same genus. All modifications of mind were simply differences of measurement. In "Éclaircissement II," Malebranche wrote that the faculties of the soul are not entities of the soul any more than extensions in length, width, and breadth are entities distinguishable from matter. Consequently, as modifications of mind, the understanding and the will were not really distinct, either from the soul or from one another within it, but comprised solely what could be termed notional distinctions of equal value.[13]

With the above in mind, Malebranche exercised great care in defining being, substance, essence, and modification. Everything that can be conceived, he argued, must be conceived either as standing alone or as dependent on some other conception: "There is no middle ground." Standing alone an object is conceived "as existing independently of some other thing, or without the idea one has of it representing some other thing," and it is "assuredly a being or a substance."[14] Every object that cannot be conceived as standing alone depends upon another and is therefore "a manner of being, or a modification of substance."[15] Only two created substances fulfill this definition of a substance: mind and matter. Particular bodies might have length, width, depth, measureable shape, movement, and other similar characteristics, but none of these characteristics can be conceived alone; all presuppose extension. Therefore, particular bodies are not substances but "modifications" or "manners of being" of extension, body in general. Extension, however, can be conceived alone because "it includes no necessary relation to other ideas."[16] Accordingly, it is a substance. Likewise, close examination of mental phenomena, such as willing, sensation, imagination, and thinking, indicates that only thought is conceived as necessary to mind: will, sensation, and imagination are all modifications of mind which assume thought. Of mental modifications thought alone is substantial: "By this word *thought*, I do not at all mean here the particular modifications of the soul, that is to say, such or such a thought, but substantial thought, the thought capable of all kinds of modifications or thoughts."[17] Thus, although retaining much of the traditional definition of substance as being that subsists in itself, Malebranche abandoned the concept of particular substances that stand alone as ontological subjects. Mind and matter were conceived only as substances in general.

It followed that essence too referred exclusively to substance in general. Defined as "what one conceives of primary significance in this thing [substance], on which depend all the modifications that one can distinguish,"[18] an essence was only notionally distinct from a substance not really distinct. A substance and its essence could even be used interchangeably. For example, he often called extension a substance and the essence of the substance, matter. Whereas only a notional distinction could be drawn between substance and essence, Malebranche did seem to recognize a greater sort of distinction between substance and modification.[19] Yet again there could be no real distinction in being as had been conceived by most scholastic thinkers. As Connell notes, substance and accident are really distinct in scholastic thought because accident is to substance as act is to potency. Inasmuch as act contributes to potency a further perfection, so does accident contribute a further perfection to substance, one it would otherwise not possess and one without which it would be imperfect and incomplete.[20] Malebranche, along with Descartes, rejected the act-potency distinction and therefore interpreted the scholastic meanings of substance and accident as though the two were independent entities, thereby reducing to absurdity the distinction since substance must be conceived as standing alone in its own right. Consequently, for Malebranche, a modification contributes no new perfection in being to substance. In effect the entire reality of a modified substance is simply the reality of the substance, constant and unalterable.[21] The upshot of his conception of substance is that, while Malebranche viewed all things that existed as either substances or modifications, the perfection of substance does not develop through its modifications but must reside in it from the outset. To account for these perfections, one cannot resort to generic classifications or discoveries made through the senses, as with the traditional model; instead, perfection must be explained totally and initially prior to any explanation of particular perfections.

The shift in Malebranche's conception of substance from the traditional, scholastic position was mirrored by his ambiguous treatment of reality. As background for a discussion of this ambiguity, it is useful to look briefly at Plato's notion of the real, a notion, writes Arthur Lovejoy, that was transmitted through the centuries in the "chain of being." The following description derives much from Lovejoy and from R. G. Collingwood. Plato's theory of forms, notes Collingwood, captured two essential ideas. Relative to the behavior of things in which it exists, form is the essence or nature of things. It gives them their peculiar properties (not merely their shapes) and reveals their differences from one another.[22] Relative to the human mind that studies nature, form is not perceptible like the things constituting the natural world, but it is intelligible. The plurality of forms constitutes what may be called an intelligible world. This intelligible world is fully real and independent and is not simply a product of the imagination or intellect. The principal meaning of "real" in this context is rendered by the term "*alethes*," which means literally unhidden or undeceptive. For instance, calling a man real connotes his candor, openness, and truthfulness about himself; he is not a hypocrite. Calling a thing real means it does not deceive us; we do not think of it as something other than what it actually is. Collingwood used the example of lace by way of illustration. When we refer to lace as real we mean it is genuine lace and not a false copy. (Or again, the realness of an antique is its authenticity as an antique; it is the genuine article.) Consequently, when Plato characterized perceptible things as unreal, he meant that they were not genuine articles not that perceptibles lacked existence.

Moreover, it was proof of the unreality or deceptiveness of things in the natural world that they are subject to change. When things show themselves to be transitory, they reveal an insecure and deceptive hold upon their own ostensible characteristics. To say that the sun is not real, for Plato, was not to deny its existence but to indicate that, as we see it, the sun is dying or changing, which is merely another way of saying that it possesses nonsolar or even antisolar features that are by degrees overcoming the solar characteristics. This contrasts with mathematical figures, such as a triangle or a circle, neither of which contains hidden elements of 'nontriangularity' or 'noncircularity'. All the elements of a triangle are present in it at all times. If they are not, there is no triangle. And as with mathematical figures, so with all ideas. Ideas are real because they are genuine and perfect; all characteristics are present in them at all times. The world of forms therefore is the truest and hence the most real,[23] contrasting with the perceptible world in which things are not so perfect. This conception of reality enabled and indeed required the gradations of perfection from the perceptible and imperfect to the real and perfect, those infinite qualitative gradations of genuineness that comprised the existence and plenitude of the great chain of being. Such perfection and genuineness gave both moral and metaphysical value to the hierarchy of 'substance'.[24]

As indicated, Malebranche's relation to this model was ambiguous. Following his characterization of modifications as degrees, "of more and less," of substances and not the addition of perfections or qualities to them, Malebranche perceived reality in a purely disjunctive sense. (The imagery here might be described as a horizontal plane, as opposed to the vertical ascendancy of the hierarchy of the chain of being.) Reality is simply what exists; unreality is nonexistence or nothingness. This conception underscored Malebranche's descriptions of truths as "real relations" and falsity as the negation of truth "or a false and imaginary relation."[25] A true relation was both real and existent. Conversely, a false relation was neither real nor did it exist. Falseness did not simply refer to imperfection but to the lack of existence itself. To say that twice two equals five is to assert a relation that does not exist and is therefore false and unreal, although we may imagine or believe it to be real. Our imagining or belief is real as a modification of mind, but the relation is not. To say that twice two is less than five, however, is to recognize a true relationship and hence a piece of reality.[26] Reality is disjunctive then because it either is or it is not. In such a formulation we can detect the influence of mathematical thinking when we recall that logicians frequently utilize the inference of "material equivalence" between the disjunctive statement $P \vee Q$ (read as 'either P or Q') and the hypothetical statement $P \supset Q$ (read as 'if P, then Q'). The exact inference is $(P \supset Q) \equiv (\sim P \vee Q)$ ('if P then Q' is true if and only if 'either not P or Q' is true.)[27] The point of this inference in the present discussion is that all disjunctive statements may be inferentially converted to hypothetical ones (and vice versa), and hypothetical statements of the type 'if . . . then', as noted earlier, embody both the form and content of mathematical statements. If such and such a relation is true of anything, then such and such another relation must also be true. In short, insofar as Malebranche's chief concern is to make reality purely disjunctive by identifying it with existence and conceiving it disjunctively with nonexistence (vis-à-vis conceiving reality as gradations of qualities), then we have good evidence for the thoroughness with which Malebranche's metaphysics was imbued with 'number'. It is accordingly a very real change in the traditional notion of substance.

A corroboration of this disjunctive sense of reality can be discerned in Malebranche's characterization of "nothingness": "Nothingness has no properties."[28] This phrase, which appears frequently in his writings, is often accompanied by a corollary, stating that, because nothingness had no properties, it was neither visible nor intelligible and, as such, was the absolute antithesis of being.[29] Neither being nor any of its parts could "enter again" into nothingness or "be elicited from nothingness."[30] Malebranche's intention with this description was to characterize nothingness as purely negative, referring to the absence of properties in contrast to being, which referred to the presence of any or all properties.[31] The identification of being with intelligibility, modification, or perception was essential: "All that is intelligible is reduced to being and the manner of being."[32] Anything thought, perceived, willed—in short any object that was either a mental modification or a substance apart from the mind (as he argued ideas were)—*is*; all else is denoted by nothingness. Either being or nothingness; substance or nonexistence.

In Malebranche's conception there is thus a shift away from Aristotle's perspective in which everything, even non-being, is reduced to the fixed point of substance and being: "There are many senses in which a thing is said to be, but all refer to one starting point," even the "negations . . . of substance itself. It is for this reason that we say even of non-being that it *is* non-being."[33] Not so for Malebranche. The fixed point is not affirmation of predicables, which assumes the copulative 'is' that joins being and non-being for Aristotle, but the hypothetical form of relating propositions, which assumes only the logical laws of noncontradiction and identity. Consequently, being and non-being cannot be related: "Nothingness and being are two terms that my mind cannot connect, and between which it can discover no relation whatsoever."[34] His inference here is a hypothetical one between propositions: if x is a modification, then x is being, and if x is being, then x is not non-being. The affirmation of x is achieved through consciousness of any ideas or modes of mental operation.[35] Consequently, Malebranche did not affirm with Aristotle that nothingness *is* non-being or anything but simply that it indicates the lack of properties—and ultimately the lack of perception or mental activity. If one has mental activity at all, it is not nothing that one thinks, wills, perceives, or senses: "One can well exist sometimes without self-reflection, but, it seems to me, one does not know how to subsist for a moment without thinking of being; and at the same time one believes he is thinking of nothing, he is necessarily filled with the vague and general idea of being."[36] In contrast to the traditional model of 'substance', Malebranche's contention was that there is no being that does not exist and that is concomitantly not real: modifications are simply a question of degree, "of more and less." With the model of 'substance', on the other hand, both being and non-being had reference to the fixed point of substance and existence, from which it was possible to derive the proposition that beings can exist without being real or perfect.[37]

While the apparent transformation of substance in Malebranche's thought outlined above reveals the impact of the 'number' model, the mathematization of 'substance', elsewhere his writings indicate a sustained effort to avoid altering the traditional descriptions of substance, reality, and perfection. To maintain continuity with tradition he invoked one of the pairs of categories distinguishing the types of relations. We have seen earlier how he separated the relations of necessity from those of contingency and the relations of magnitude from those of quality and perfection. Of these dichotomies, the latter was the more significant: "But one can distinguish in God two kinds of truths or relations: relations of magnitude and relations of perfection; speculative truths and practical truths; relations that exact only judgments by their evidence and others that stimulate the emotions."[38] Whereas the truths of magnitude were "speculative" or scientific (he usually considered metaphysics and mathematics in this regard as equal kinds of necessary truths), the truths of perfection were chiefly practical. Their sphere of operation was not in the pure intellect but rather in the will, the sense, and the imagination. Accordingly they could be classed also as truths of quality—all relations other than those of magnitude. They are practical insofar as they govern the actions of the soul and "the emotions of the heart."[39] Although apparently contingent, relations of perfection are not fortuitous, chaotic, or subjective, but are impressed by God upon the heart in an orderly fashion and thus direct it to return to the highest end, absolute love, which resides exclusively with God. In other words, God impresses upon men the general direction of man's will, toward "the undetermined and general good."[40] Relations of perfection were thus seen as constituting the prescriptive moral law and divine justice that lead man to this end—God's eternal order: "Law consists only of the eternal and immutable order of divine perfections."[41]

If there were relations of perfection, then it followed for Malebranche that these were also qualities, greater and lesser perfections, graduated into a hierarchy of realities. (Indeed, insofar as all beings were particular, they could not possess the unconditioned and general perfection of the goodness of God.) One could know something of these lesser qualities, for knowledge of relations of perfection and imperfection was based upon the same cognitive principle as knowledge of clear and distinct ideas. The fullest development of the similar epistemic basis for relations of perfection and magnitude emerged in Malebranche's treatment of the self or soul. In the preface to the *Recherche*, Malebranche had written that "the most beautiful, pleasing, and necessary of all knowledge is, without doubt, knowledge of ourselves."[42] After a lengthy examination of the nature of knowledge, however, he was forced to conclude, in sharp contrast to Descartes, that such knowledge was less than perfect since man could never have a clear and distinct idea of the soul. There were, he had shown, four types of knowledge: knowledge of God, which is direct; knowledge of material objects, which is mediated through ideas; knowledge of the self, which is conscience or "inner feeling"; and knowledge of other selves, which is founded exclusively on conjecture.[43] There could be no clear and distinct idea of the soul because one could not know with exactitude the relations between mental modifications, such as perceptions, sensations, and volitions, in the same manner that one could know the exact relations between proportions of extension. It was possible to know *that* modifications of mind were merely differences of degree but not *what* those differences were. In His wisdom, Malebranche wrote, God had not found it fitting to reveal to man the archetype or nature of spiritual beings; if He had, man would be able to know feelings such as pain without ever having experienced them and would be like God. The result was that man's "substance, far from becoming clear, is in itself unintelligible to him,"[44] and despite the assertion that knowledge of self is the most beautiful, pleasing, and necessary, men "cannot discover the truth in self-contemplation."[45]

But if one could not know with exactitude the truth, the modifications of the soul, nor as a consequence possess a clear and distinct idea of the soul, he could nonetheless with a certitude equal to that of his knowledge of clear and distinct ideas know *that* the soul existed. For both types of cognition had the same basis. We recall Malebranche's first principle in the *Recherche*, upon which he constructed his theory of mathematical truths. The principle stated that one should never consent to propositions unless they appear so true that to refuse to acknowledge them would prompt "an inner pain and the secret reproaches of reason."[46] Later on in Book VI of the *Recherche*, he employed the same principle as the basis for knowledge of the self's existence through "inner feeling," or, as he also termed it, through knowledge "by simple view." One can know that the soul exists because he can and indeed must consent to the propositions "I think" and "I am" "without suffering the secret reproaches of his reason." In this same passage he indicated that in addition to the propositions "I think" and "I am," knowledge by "simple view" established the truth of the proposition $2 \times 2 = 4$, implying clearly that the truths of reason or magnitude and those of the soul's existence and its activity, truths of perfection, were equally incontestable: "The first of all our cognitions is the existence of our soul; all our thoughts are indisputable demonstrations of it; for nothing is more evident than what actually thinks is something."[47] One must, therefore, accept the soul's existence even though one did not possess a clear and distinct idea of it.

Yet because we have no clear and distinct idea of the soul, our knowledge of what it is remains imperfect and incomplete knowledge. We can know *that* a man thinks, or *that* a man is, from the performance of the mental acts that assume the soul as the "I who thinks, feels, wills,"[48] although we cannot know the exact nature of the feeling or thinking or willing.[49] The imperfect nature of our knowledge of the soul is significant because through it is established the close connection between imperfection and perfection. Indeed, despite the differences in Descartes' and Malebranche's understanding of the soul, there is a common acceptance of this relation as a key to the question of man's relation to God. But the archetypes framing the two conceptions of this relation were reversed. Descartes had contended that we know clearly and distinctly what the soul is; it is a thinking substance, a 'unit', but an imperfect unit because of the doubt that produced it. From this he derived perfection and hence God on the model of 'number'. Malebranche gave this argument a twist and shifted models by claiming not a perfect knowledge of the soul's imperfection but an imperfect knowledge of the soul itself, from which with equal certitude he could infer perfection and God on the basis of 'substance'. Malebranche concluded that "true, the knowledge we have of our soul by conscience is imperfect, but it is not at all false."[50] With this conclusion Malebranche revealed his traditional and Platonic colors. Imperfect but not false; knowledge of the soul establishes the soul and its reality. Its reality, however, is imperfection, and reality here is thus not disjunctive but graduated on the qualitative scale of higher and lower forms of genuineness, authenticity, and perfection.

In the *Traité de morale*, Malebranche made explicit this qualitative hierarchy. There he argued that objects are ordered with respect to their qualitative valuations:

> It is true that a beast is more estimable than a stone and less estimable than a man, because there is a greater perfection in the beast relative to the stone than in the stone relative to the beast, and because there is a lesser perfection in the beast compared to the man than in the man compared to the beast. And he who sees these relations of perfection sees truths that ought to govern his esteem, and, consequently, this type of love that the esteem brings about.[51]

The inequalities between a rock and a beast, and between a beast and a man, are not simply differences of measurement, not different collections of number or extension units of equal value. They are inequalities indicative of greater or less value, esteem or perfection. A man possesses greater perfection than a beast, a beast greater perfection than a rock. Perfections and their relations constitute collectively God's generic order, of which the soul's awareness of its own imperfect knowledge is one of the first discoveries.[52] Man can know these relations because of his finite and limited understanding and because God has given him "the feelings of inner approval or reproach through which this [divine] reason consoles [men] when they obey this law [God's eternal order of perfections], or torments them when they do not obey it."[53]

Truths of magnitude then and truths of perfection are distinct from one another to the discerning mind of man.[54] Each constitutes its own sphere of being. Truths of magnitude are the eternal and objective ideas, the real relations, that exist in God as His substance and hence as His word. Truths of perfection reside in the created order, within both the substances of matter and of mind, and govern the relations between bodies and between mental modifications. Truths of magnitude are clearly mathematical, and when Malebranche describes them as real, he describes reality in a mathematical manner as disjunctive. The truths of perfections are also real but in a different sense. Their reality is qualitative and hierarchical, very closely allied to the chain of being, and involving both God's sufficient reason and plenitude of goodness.[55] Such truths as expressions of God's will are immutable and necessary, though their necessity cannot be known exactly. Being, then, is ambiguously described under the influence of 'number' as well as under the influence of the archetype of 'substance'.

But if these descriptions were to be clearly distinguished in man's mind, Malebranche continued to urge that in God's mind they were not. "*Truth* and *order* are real relations of magnitude and perfection, immutable and necessary, relations included in the substance of the Divine Word."[56] Were man to know as much as God, he would find that all relations of perfection and quality would be as exact as the relations of magnitude. That man does not see all truths of perfection in an exact manner is simply reflective of man's ontological nature—his qualitative imperfection. He sees some hierarchical truths and qualitative differences because of his own limitations. This is why his knowledge of these truths is through conscience or inner feeling and is thereby limited though not false. Nonetheless, even for man, Malebranche claimed, there is a potential isomorphic similarity between the two types of realities. And the more one progresses in knowledge, the more exact all relations of inequality will become. Consequently, the inequalities in relations of perfection that are all qualitative differences, as for example the inequality between a man and a beast or between an image and a sensation, could potentially be known with exactitude. All perfections then could potentially be reduced to the real truths of magnitude: "Nevertheless, relations of perfection cannot be clearly known if they are not expressed by relations of magnitude."[57] One would know not only that the soul existed but would then have a clear and distinct idea of it and of the exact, that is, quantitatively established, relations between it and all its modifications—in the same way one has a clear and distinct idea of the exact relations between all ideas and correspondingly between all modifications of material extension. All perceptions then of perfections and qualitative distinctions would be simply immediate perceptions of Being itself.[58] And the apparent hierarchy of classes of mental objects, which is yet real though imperfect, would melt completely into the infinite Being of God: substance transformed into mathematics; mathematics made substantial.

Thus in Malebranche's treatment of substance, reality, and perfection, there existed a tension between the traditional model and the emerging one of 'number', between the desire to maintain the qualitatively pure and the quantitatively exact. The most significant implication of this tension was to alter many of the traditional means for treating being-in-general. On the model of 'substance', being-in-general could have meaning only through the support of individual existents classed by their general and specific characteristics, which revealed the unfolding of metaphysical substrata and differentia. On this model, the more general the concept, the more perfection and reality it contained and exhibited. On the model of 'number', however, the entire problem of substance and being centered not on the problem of the individual existents and their relations with one another, and to the higher modes of being, but solely on the question of being-in-general.[59] To support being-in-general without reference to classified particular beings, Malebranche consequently was forced to develop arguments that departed from the traditional pattern of 'substance' yet bore close relation to the traditional assumptions of 'substance'. These arguments are the topic of the next chapter.

CHAPTER 6

Assumptions of 'Substance'

As a metaphysical expression of God, Being-in-General (or simply Being) was pivotal for Malebranche. It included all truths of magnitude and perfection, and its grounding, used to establish God's existence, was of epistemological and religious importance. In his discussions of Being and particularly with the most famous and frequent of his proofs of God, the "proof by simple view," Malebranche revealed his attachment to traditional natural theology and to the model of 'substance', although with some alterations. We shall see in this chapter four distinct assumptions at the base of his metaphysics, and thus his religious thought, that indicate this attachment: (1) the ontological priority of Infinite Being that imposes itself upon thought; (2) the corollary premise that thought reflects principally upon Being, rather than upon itself; (3) a perfection and infinity viewed as positive and intuited not privative and assumed; and (4) a metaphysical substratum that unfolds itself in the created substances of mind and matter, a substratum discernible because of the transitive causation presupposed in the theory of occasionalism.

Assumptions of 'Substance'

In one sense Malebranche's "proof by simple view" can be seen as a compression of Descartes' *cogito*, although this observation might initially appear incongruous. How could anyone compress such a simple, pristine, powerful statement, one that does not seem to suffer from excess? Yet, when we recall that the full meaning of the *cogito* becomes evident only when joined with the inference, "I exist, therefore God exists," the observation is justified. For Malebranche postulated a single, direct intuition that establishes God and all Being and man's relation to Being insofar as it can be known. The proof of God then is expressed simply: "If one thinks of Him, He must be."[1] A variation reads: "It suffices to think of God to know that He is."[2] As put forth in this formula, knowledge of God's existence is direct and unmediated by ideas or by any existents in the world. Man knows God, Malebranche held, through an "immediate union that we have with the Word of God, sovereign Reason,"[3] not as the result of any inferential process. Such knowledge is a form of ontologism in theological terms. (In fact, he claimed that inferential knowledge of God is spurious.[4]) Consequently, to speak of inferences when discussing his proof of God is somewhat misleading. Like knowledge of our soul's existence, knowledge of God's existence "by simple view" is a feature of human consciousness. Nonetheless, Malebranche intended more than dogma in this assertion, and although no inferences could establish God's existence definitively, certain observations and arguments could be proffered to make the direct view more comprehensible.

Malebranche articulated man's direct and unmediated relation to God in two principal fashions: the vision of things *in* God and the vision *of* God. In the first of these formulations, man has direct union with ideas, which are real and which are God's substance inasmuch as it represents material bodies. The purely intelligible ideas we receive (which he had earlier called pure perceptions) differ ontologically from the ideas that are modifications of the soul's substance. Malebranche was led to argue for the existence of pure ideas as real and exterior in order to explain how mind could know matter without having an essential likeness with matter or without being caused by it. Since bodies could not cause the contents of the mind (which merely corresponded to bodies in a one-to-one fashion according to God's laws of conjunction), it followed that to make any cognitive claim about bodies at all required the intermediary of independent ideas. The existence of ideas was initially described as a plurality of intelligible substances in the first edition of the *Recherche*. However, under criticism from Foucher and later from Arnauld, this ideal existence came to be characterized by the concept of intelligible extension, as we saw earlier.[5] On this reading, intelligibility is God's wisdom or reason or the "Word," through which God is able to know matter without actually being consubstantial with it. Since man can know matter only through the relations of intelligible extension, all man's knowledge of nature is knowledge of things through God's ideas. Man's direct union with these ideas is thus an unmediated apprehension of the mathematical relations that exist apart from both mind and matter and hence is a direct union with God Himself.

From man's perspective, this direct union must be finite because of the mind's finitude. The mind always grasps specific, finite relations, even between infinities, as in the case of comprehending relations between incommensurables.[6] The incommensurables are infinite; the relations between them are not. One never comprehends infinity in mathematics but only finite relations and procedures that, when repeated, will lead to it. From the comprehension of finite relations, the mind is led to conceive its necessary union with the infinite itself, just as *unité* necessarily embraces infinity. This infinity is not merely privative, not just the indefinite repetition of acts of thought, but the necessary and positive end of thought. We know it to exist not because we see precisely what it is (or comprehend it), nor solely because we cannot imagine an end to thinking, but because we must recognize that infinity is presupposed *as* the end of our thinking:

> No, Ariste, the mind does not see an infinite extension in the sense that its thought or its perception equals an infinite extension. If this were so it would comprehend it and would itself be infinite. For a thought must be infinite in order to measure an infinite idea, in order to be actually united with all that the infinite comprehends. But the *mind actually sees that its immediate object is infinite*; it actually sees that intelligible extension is infinite. And not, as you think, because it does not see the end of it, . . . but because it sees clearly that [extension] has no end at all.[7]

To assert *that* there is no end to intelligible extension is a positive assertion of the infinite reality of the relations of intelligible extension. Schematized, the argument is as follows: (1) All that a mind sees has properties (is substance or modification); were this not true the mind would not see. (2) The relations a mind sees are finite because the mind itself is finite, and the finite cannot contain the infinite. (3) These finite relations are real and independent of the mind; they are thus positive realities. (4) We can assert with certitude that infinity is the natural limit to the number of positive, finite relations. (5) We can be assured then of a positive infinity. (6) This positive infinity is God. (7) Therefore in seeing things through idea relations, we see them through God and are directly united to Him, even though we cannot comprehend Him entirely.[8] Thus, we can know *that* infinity exists positively without knowing what it is, just as we can know *that* the soul exists without knowing exactly its nature.

In effect Malebranche's ontological description of intelligible extension served to hypostatize the relations of 'number' in considering them as God's word or reason. Man's connection with this reason is direct and intimate. When the mind grasps God's word it receives mathematical relations, and its reception of these ideas assumes them as ontologically prior to thought. Infinite Being acts upon thought insofar as man sees all things through its relations. The vision *in* God thus relies on the assumption of an ontologically prior Being, the necessary source of the relations one perceives, relations that exist not only as representative of all actually existing material bodies but of all possible ones as well.

Besides the vision of all things in God, Malebranche described man's direct relation to God in a second manner. This was the vision *of* God, and here direct vision referred to the reception of the idea of God itself. This idea was like any other idea in that "one ought to attribute to a thing what is clearly conceived to be included in the idea that represents it." Inasmuch as the idea of God represents God, there is the question as to what can be clearly conceived in this idea. Malebranche answered that the idea of God represents "an infinitely perfect being."[9] Through several passages in different works he repeated and clarified these terms. Infinity, he wrote, is an attribute of God and in fact "His essential attribute."[10] It is universal and positive because it includes all other attributes: "The infinity in all kinds of perfections is an attribute of divinity, and its essential attribute, the one that includes all others."[11] Since substance and essence are interchangeable, as was seen with the case of matter and extension, Infinity, as the essence of God, is also His metaphysical equivalent. The same is true of Being. Being is described as both the essence of God and that which designates Him: "Moreover, you see what God is, since God and Being, or the infinite, are only the same thing."[12] Consequently, to conceive the idea of Infinity or Being is to envision God Himself.

Furthermore, there was with the idea of God a "simplicity"

of essence. Besides implying an infinity of perfections, the idea of God referred to God's property of being one, simple, undifferentiated, complete: "It is a property of Infinite Being to be one and, in a sense, all things; that is to say, perfectly simple, without any composition of parts, realities, perfections, and capable of being imitated or imperfectly participated in by different beings in an infinite number of ways."[13] Malebranche repeated the same view elsewhere, noting that one of the properties of the Infinite is to "comprehend all" and "remain simple."[14] Insofar as He can be conceived, God must be complex and infinite, possessing all truths and perfections, yet He must remain simple and undivided, complete in Himself. The affinity of this description with the properties of 'number' is all too striking, and reinforces Malebranche's hypostatization of mathematical truths as the highest mode of knowable reality. God is both singular, undifferentiated, and simple—*unité* in its metaphysical meaning—and complex and general, metaphysical infinity. The idea of God revealed the oneness of unit and the completeness of unity—the discreteness and continuity of 'number'. Confirmation of this point issues from the identification in God of the truths of perfection with those of magnitude, so that all qualitative distinctions in Him are reduced to a necessity at once logical and metaphysical. This too suggests a reason for Malebranche's general emphasis on God's infinity over His perfection. Malebranche did infer other metaphysical attributes from the idea of the infinitely perfect Being, including perfect wisdom, power, and goodness, as traditionally formulated. But these attributes were, in a sense, all secondary adjuncts to God's essence insofar as man could conceive it most clearly. Just as one could conceive the truths of magnitude and its infinity more clearly than the truths of perfection, so too did God's infinity appear to the mind as the clearest attribute of His being. In short, to speak with any clarity, albeit limited, about God, one must penetrate the concept of an infinitely perfect Being: "One must be raised in mind above all creatures and, with a great deal of attention and respect, consult the vast and immense idea of infinitely perfect Being."[15]

The idea of an infinitely perfect Being as representative of God was not new in Malebranche's day. It had, in fact, a lengthy history in natural theology. (Some Christian apologists would say it dated from the third chapter of Exodus.) Even though his mathematical instincts led him to interpret the notion in a somewhat novel manner, his general characterization of these metaphysical attributes of God tied him firmly to both the Platonic and Aristotelian traditions of the Middle Ages. Never reluctant to use ideas from his predecessors when he thought they were valuable, Malebranche endeavored in his synthesizing efforts to maintain continuity with the past. Thus he held, in full accord with tradition, that Being connotes neither any created thing, nor the essence of any created thing, but only the Divine itself or the essence of the Divine.[16] All particular beings participate in Being, but no particular being can be its equal. Being comprises all things, but all beings, created or possible, in all their manifest variety, could never exhaust its immense extension. Malebranche viewed his own identification of intelligible extension with the "Word" as a description of this idea so central to natural theology: "But is God this intelligible extension? Yes, certainly for all that is in God is God himself. This intelligible extension is wisdom, is power, is infinitely perfect: not as it is representative of bodies, not as we see it, understanding only the eternal idea of creatures, but according to its substance, which we do not see in itself."[17] God is His own substance, which man cannot fully know but which is present in the idea of Infinite Being. As its own idea, Infinite Being was not subject to any archetype or higher idea; it simply contained within itself the pattern of all created beings.[18] Existing in and by itself alone, it is the highest ontological principle, and thus it is established by the efficacy of its own nature not by man's thought. Malebranche's phrase is exact and telling: "One can see the infinite only in itself and *only by the efficacy of its substance*."[19] It is God's actual existence that renders the idea of Infinite Being as representative of His essence both possible and necessary. As Descartes phrased it, "The necessity of the existence of God determines [one] to think this way."[20] Therefore "if one thinks of the infinite, it must be" is true not from any epistemological considerations per se but because the infinite, divine substance imposes itself upon thought in a necessary fashion.

Moreover, with Malebranche the inference of God's existence from the concept of being was not, to head off Kant, the addition of one idea to another but an inference of a different order. Malebranche referred specifically to Descartes' example of the mountain and the valley to make a distinction between purely notional or analytical relations and those that are ontological. While it is impossible analytically that a mountain could exist without a valley, it is equally impossible, ontologically, that the infinitely perfect Being does not exist. Being exists, not just because the predicates of infinity or perfection are joined to its idea, but because "necessary existence is included in the idea of the infinite."[21] Necessary existence, not the *idea* of necessary existence, is implied by the infinitely perfect Being. In other words, the predicates of being, perfection, and infinity are joined to the subject God because of God's actual existence and as a reflection or revelation of His metaphysical reality. As "an infinite substance"[22] God unfolds himself, as it were, to the receptive mind in and through essential predication. This inference again reveals the assumption of an ontological priority so fundamental to the archetype of 'substance'.

This assumption of an ontological priority and its infinite perfections bore a close relation to Anselm's second form of the ontological argument. Anselm had stressed that necessary existence is the only mode of being appropriate to the idea of God as perfection. Abbreviated grossly, the argument is that, for the idea of God to be consistent, it must include His necessary existence. What gave this argument its force was a conception of perfection similar to Plato's, which was described earlier. The scale of perfections was coterminous with the scale of being; the more perfect or genuine any object was, the more being it possessed. Either in its pure state or in any of its lesser modes, perfection required existence in order to be intelligible. To say of a man that he is a real person, meaning that he is candid and honest, would be wholly unintelligible were this simply adding one idea to another. A man reveals himself as real only in existence. Likewise with a perfect triangle: it is revealed as real and authentic because it includes all qualities necessary to its existence as a perfectly real triangle. Thus, for Anselm and also for Malebranche, insofar as God is Infinite Perfection, He must exist; to speak otherwise is unintelligible.[23] Gilson states the point succinctly: with God, "there exists a being whose intrinsic necessity is such as to be reflected in the very idea we form of Him."[24]

In the heritage of Neoplatonism traversing Augustine, Anselm, and Bonaventure, and grounding these arguments, being is thus not a logical category but an ontological one.[25] And that being exists is not at all an epistemological or logical question, as E. L. Mascall writes: "If a necessary being exists, it does so not in obedience to a logical demonstration, but because its very nature is such as to maintain it in existence, because, if we may venture to use the expression, it keeps going under its own ontological steam."[26] A most explicit formulation of this idea is found in the *Recherche*: "It is evident that being (I do not say a *particular being*) has its existence by itself and that being cannot not actually be, being impossible and contradictory that true being is without existence."[27] Behind this passage is the complex and traditional inference from possible being to the necessity of necessary being. To conceive the possibility of being as not existing implies the idea of possible being, being that can or cannot exist. This disjunction is viable only when being that has no possibility of not existing is invoked to explain the eduction of being that can exist into actually existent being. But being that has no possibility of not existing is simply another way of stating necessary being. In short, from the idea of possible being follows a necessary inference to necessary being. Hence even the mere possibility of God, which we derive from the thought of infinity or from the idea of God, presupposed His prior existence.[28] Here Malebranche is in full accord with the tradition of natural theology.

Further evidence that Malebranche's conception of God as Infinite Being was traditional and based on the assumptions of 'substance' is reflected in its affinity with Aquinas' position that God's being transcends any categories, that He can be neither a genus nor a species. St. Thomas held that being cannot be differentiated. If being were a genus, then it must have differentia (modifications), which determine the genus to the species contained within it. If it has differentia then these cannot be members of the same genus. For example, in the case of 'man is a rational animal', man is of the genus 'animal' and the species 'rational'. The modification 'rational' cannot be contained in the genus 'animal', for then there would be nothing to differentiate man from any other animals. But, continued Aquinas, every difference must be an instance of being or else it would be nonexistent, a principle to which Malebranche adhered rigorously. Therefore being cannot be a genus or, as Malebranche expressed it, being can have no modifications: "It is everything that is."[29] Aquinas, of course, went on to argue that the only knowledge of God or of Being was analogical, a doctrine Malebranche did not accept, holding that the immediate union of the soul to God did not require the mediation of analogy.[30]

Maritain has outlined the ontological priority present in substantive theology and maintained by Malebranche: "What is primarily known . . . is being. But nothing can be added to it extrinsically to differentiate it, for all differentiations issue from its own depths, as some one or other of its own modes."[31] Without losing sight of the change in Malebranche's conception of logic or of his ambiguous treatment of reality, it is clear that for him all knowledge is of Being, and all manifestations of Being—ideas in God, real substances of mind and matter, even the purely notional relations, as, for example, between substance and essence—proceed from the depths of Being itself.[32] "All Christian and medieval philosophy [Malebranche included] must be regarded as one in *affirming* the metaphysical primacy of being, and its sequel, the identity of essence and existence in God."[33]

Beyond the assumed ontological priority of Being, whose positive and infinite perfection imposes itself upon thought, Malebranche invoked the idea of transitive, or creationist causation to describe God and His activity in the world.[34] In discussing God as transitive Creator in a dual sense, as the cause of all that is, the created substances of mind and matter, and as the cause of His own idea, Malebranche altered the notion of an unqualified causal primacy that Descartes had attributed to God. Descartes, we recall, had stressed the complete freedom of God to create or not to create. God had freely made a creation that was rational and exhibited necessity in nature, but He could have done otherwise. In Descartes' phrase, God willed necessity, but He did not will necessarily. The idea of a totally free creation without prior rational considerations was nonsense to Malebranche. True, there was no necessity in God's creation of the sensible, physical world, and in fact God's creation of it could not be established with certainty but rested on faith.[35] (Aquinas too had argued similarly that first creation could not be established on principles of natural reason but only on faith.) In this regard then God was totally free; but it did not follow that He was free to create chaos, to be irrational or indifferent. Descartes claimed that had He so desired, God could have made two plus two equal five. This was inconceivable for Malebranche, for it was inconceivable that God could act without knowledge or without motive.[36] To be sui generis, the cause of his own being or cause of necessity, without necessarily accounting for the wisdom and reason that were His, was unreasonable.[37] A God so conceived would be one who acted in a purely arbitrary fashion and would thus be somewhat insane—an implication not lost on the materialists of the eighteenth century.[38] Consequently, insofar as God was the cause of His own idea, His own idea was merely an expression of the intrinsic ontological necessity and rationality that constituted a portion of God's being. To speak of transitive causation in the creation of the objective idea of the Infinitely Perfect Being was thereby to distinguish in reason, or notionally, what could not be distinguished in reality. God was the cause of the idea of the Infinitely Perfect Being but only in the sense that the ontological reality resided fully and indistinguishably in both cause and effect. This indeed was the true meaning of cause.[39] The idea of God as Being, Perfect, and Infinite, required the cause or creation of the conception as a necessary part of the Perfection and Infinity, and hence the ontological priority was clothed fully in Reason and Necessity.

Even more than with the concept of God per se, the idea of transitive causation was instrumental in describing God's activity in the world. Malebranche accepted as axiomatic the scholastic principle *ex nihilo nihil fit* that there are no beings that have not been created or brought into being. Thus the senses and imagination are real because they exist as modifications of mind, and therefore they must have been created. Likewise, movement and the conjunctions between bodies must have been caused or created since these are modifications of matter. But neither matter nor the mind can create its own modifications. In fact, nothing in nature is able to do this because a true cause is "a cause that acts by its own force,"[40] and neither matter nor mind is capable of so acting.[41] Matter does not generate its own motion, nor does a man's mind generate its own thoughts, inclinations, and passions. Consequently, there is no necessity between any conjunctions of bodies, between a volition and subsequent bodily movement, nor between bodily movement and an idea in the mind. In none of these particular instances is there cause acting through its own force. For a true cause to occur, there must be a discernible metaphysical relation between the cause and its effect, a condition that is met only in the will of God: "There is a necessary connection between the will of God and the thing he wills."[42] The reality of the effect is present in the cause in the case of God's willing, and hence an ontological necessity may be discerned between God and the totality of His creation, between Being and all beings, a necessity that cannot be so established within any of His creatures or on any particular basis. Otherwise stated, no created thing can act upon another through an activity that is purely its own.[43] Only God can bring into being movement in bodies or inclinations in souls; only God is, properly speaking, force. To recognize this is to perceive both the lack of necessity in relations between contingent created bodies and between body and soul; and to recognize the dependency all created beings, mental or material, have upon God for the creation and perpetuation of the natural order.

This notion of cause is the underlying ground for occasionalism as Malebranche developed it. Following Descartes he contended that motion was simply translation of body from one place to another, with each translation in the plenum of the universe requiring other instantaneous changes of location. Two

laws governed motion: the law of inertia and the conservation of motion.[44] The former expressed God's will that bodies
should act as simply as possible, moving in a straight line
unless acted upon by another body. The latter was the foundation for kinematics, a description of the changes in direction as
moving bodies struck one another. Each instance of a body
striking another was an occasion in which God's will created
the sum of movement and direction and re-created it at a subsequent instant. As motion could be analysed into a succession
of instants, so also could inclination and volition.[45] God has
willed that when man exercises his will, to move his arm for
example, the act of willing (a mental act) is followed by a
bodily motion, the moving of the arm. Similarly, when the
brain receives a trace from nerves that have been stimulated by
an external body, such as a stick striking the arm, there follows
in the mind an idea, in this case a sensation of pain. All these
instances of God's willing reveal that it is only God's willful
activity that prevents chaos and establishes order in the universe: "Therefore, God has willed, and he wills without ceas-
ing, that the various perturbations of the brain are always
followed by various thoughts of the mind to which it is joined.
And it is this constant and efficacious will of the Creator that
properly makes the union of these two substances. For there is
no other nature, I wish to say, nor any other natural laws than
the Almighty's efficacious acts of will."[46] Without the efficacious will of God to create and maintain at each instant the conjunction of mind and body, or of body and body, no order at
all could be ascertained; no correspondence between thoughts
and actions could be discovered; no natural laws governing
bodies could be established.

Malebranche scholars have frequently commented that his
conception of occasionalism glosses the two toughest issues:
first, God's laws as they apply in particular to specific phenomena; second, the necessity of God's acting in accordance

with the movement of created bodies. It is surely one thing to hold, as Malebranche did, that everything occurs because God so wills it, and quite another to offer some useful criteria or means for distinguishing which of God's particular conjunctions, as perceived by man, are in fact true or not. In other words, at least for science, it was the "occasion," or patterns of similar occasions, not the absolute and universal will behind it that became the more important fact to establish.[47] Historically Malebranche often relied, as indeed did Descartes, on the results of experiments for the demonstrations of particular applications of God's two laws,[48] and in his later years he even yielded ground on the two laws, although how much his position altered has been a matter of dispute.[49] For now, it is not the practical question but the theoretical one that is significant, and here Malebranche never wavered. For efficient causation to exist, God's will had to be invoked as an explanatory principle.

But the theoretical question too did not escape difficulties. Since the conjunction of any particular bodies, or of mind and body, is the occasion for God's universal willing, one direct implication is that God's willing must occur when bodies meet and interact with one another. This has the apparent effect of making God Himself limited necessarily by the laws of His own creation, of asserting that finite things have the capacity to determine how God's will produces effects on any given occasion.[50] Malebranche countered this contention by resorting to the idea of God's omnipotence and the necessity contained therein. To hold that a necessary connection between a cause and its effects is discernible in God's will is another way of stating that an omnipotent will cannot fail to produce what it wills. Omnipotence in other words is necessarily efficacious. Hence from the omnipotent act of will, all effects, that is everything that occurs in the universe, must follow. Given this formulation the converse is likewise true: from any or all effects in the universe, one can legitimately infer to a universal cause, God's will. Of course Hume later challenged precisely this position in the eighteenth century, and he challenged it on its clearly held metaphysical foundation—the notion of creationist or transitive causation.[51]

In fact Malebranche himself paved the way for Hume's attack, for even though one could know that an omnipotent will was necessarily efficacious, it did not follow, the Oratorian claimed, that man could know what the divine will was nor that there was any such thing as a clear and distinct idea of power or efficacy.[52] Just as one could know *that* the soul existed without having a clear and distinct idea of it, or could know *that* infinity existed without comprehending it, or could know *that* God existed without knowing clearly what or who He is, so too could one know *that* God's will was omnipotent, *that* omnipotence implied the necessary relation between cause and effect, and *that* this relation underscored all events in the universe, without knowing the content of God's will in particular. Such knowledge was not founded on purely epistemic principles but presupposed an efficacious order and reality of Being that imposed itself necessarily upon thought, a presupposition that lay at the heart of 'substance'. God's substance forces one to recognize these truths and thus provides the general end and central purpose for all thinking: thought reflecting upon Being.

It is evident from the material presented in these last two chapters that the submerged model of 'substance' continued to be influential in Malebranche's thought although the model itself was changed in some significant ways. No longer was there a multiplicity of created substances but only two, mind and matter. Nor were the modifications within each of these classified by their genus and difference; rather all modifications of both mind and matter were differences of degree, of more and less, even though it was not within man's province to know all these differences with exactitude (at least in the case of mind). When one did not have exact knowledge of differences, as with the difference between imagination and sensation, a hierarchy was employed to describe the differences, but it was not a hierarchy that could be known with clarity or distinctness. The same was true with perfections. One could recognize the various levels of perfection and the qualitatively distinct levels of beings, but this knowledge was not clear and distinct. Indeed, in God's mind such classifications were eliminated, with His perfection connoting both complete reality or authenticity and exactitude. All being then was ultimately reduced to God's Being and the two types of beings He had created. The actions of created substances in all their attributes—mind and its modifications of will and understanding; matter and its modifications of figure and configuration—revealed an unfolding of metaphysical significance and revealed God's will in the world, just as the terms genus and species had revealed the unfolding reality of being and attribute in traditional thought.

Finally, underscoring the model of 'substance' in Malebranche's thought was the central assumption of 'substance'—that Being was necessary and imposed itself upon thought and that thought therefore reflected principally upon Being. The Oratorian held firmly to the distinction between the "*ordo essendi*, the order in which things ultimately exist, and the *ordo cognoscendi*, the order in which we come to know them,"[53] and to the derivation of the latter from the former. Although extant, the central assumption of 'substance' was not without difficulty, for the question emerged of whether the assumption of an ontological priority does not beg the entire issue. What sense can be derived from the claim that all that is must be either substance or attribute when the only secure foundation for making this claim, that is, knowing if this is the case, is a propositional or relational, vis-à-vis generic, mode of abstraction. The ontological assumption in other words traditionally requires in some sense a classificatory mode of abstraction for support. Being is empty and meaningless without beings. When the introduction of Being to a relational mode of abstraction serves merely to hypostatize mathematical relations, to consider them real, then such relations in and of themselves cannot be employed to ground Being but can only provide a description of necessity between its parts. The ontological priority thus appears wholly gratuitous. The essential question in this dilemma, and indeed the central question of the tension between science and religion in Malebranche's thought, was whether or not first principles were to be ontological or epistemological, whether or not primacy was to be granted to 'substance' or to 'number'. To this tension we must now turn.

CHAPTER 7

The Conflict between 'Substance' and 'Number'

The persistence in Malebranche's writings of two distinct patterns or submerged models of thought—one traditional, 'substance'; one new and emergent, 'number'—is by now well documented. There remains to examine how the tension between these formal patterns of thought affected his understanding of the relation between science and religion. That the new science would affect religion and theology was immediately manifest. Descartes himself had no doubt about this when he wrote Mersenne in 1630 that the destruction of Aristotelian physics would require theologians to reexamine the traditional doctrine of the eucharist.[1] Malebranche initially welcomed the epistemological innovations of 'number' and the resultant mind-body metaphysics as a positive achievement for theology which freed the soul from reliance on senses and the body. In his estimation the new science would lend greater support to the existence of the soul and its survival upon separation from the body at death. The mind-body 'problem', generally speaking, did not present so much a problem for Malebranche as it did a clearer illumination of some long-standing religious truths.[2] His exuberance was not unqualified, however, as some of the implications of 'number' began to be elicited both by himself and his critics. Although he labored tirelessly to ally Catholic thought and natural theology with the new science, the result can only be seen as ironical, leading to an increased anxiety within theology and a greater scepticism that science and religion could be brought together. In Malebranche we find an intellectual and spiritual tension that further belies the myth of "the serenity of the 'glorious classical age'." As Henri Gouhier writes, "Throughout the 17th century, the Catholic soul is an anxious soul"[3]—and with reason.

How then did epistemic innovations, the emergence of new assumptions and inferences, materially influence older and established conceptions? How did the new wineskins affect the old wine? In answering this it is useful to concentrate first on the conflict between models as exhibited in three of the concepts traditionally viewed as attributes of God: infinity, necessity, being. From this the shift in modes of logical description as pertaining to God, and thus as grounding natural theology, will become more apparent. Finally, the unresolved tension between reason and faith, between science and religion, will emerge and with it the irony in Malebranche's desire to see clearly and believe blindly.

The meaning and significance of infinity for Malebranche, both as an attribute of God and as a pivotal concept in mathematics, have been amply illustrated. The thrust of his position was generally toward a conception of the two meanings as mutually inclusive (if one thinks of infinity, it exists). Accordingly, to demonstrate the necessity of infinity in mathematics was to prove it existed and to support the inference that God existed as well. This inference, however, was not a logical necessity. Infinity, he often remarked, could only be conceived not comprehended.[4] One could never know what it was, only that it was. In mathematics this meant that infinity itself was never grasped with exactitude. One comprehended the finite relations between infinities but only conceived that certain operations and functions led necessarily to infinity.

> The mind sees clearly that the number, which when multiplied by itself produces 5 or some other number between 4 and 9, 9 and 16, 16 and 25, etc., is a magnitude, a relation, a fraction whose terms have more figures than there can be from one pole of the world to the other. It sees clearly that it is a relation only God can comprehend, and that it is impossible to express it exactly because one would have to express a fraction whose two terms are infinite.[5]

The justification for the claim that such fractions led necessarily to infinity, which only God could comprehend, was found in the process of reasoning by recurrence, the repetition of a mental act ad infinitum. The continuity assumed by mathematical induction led to the claim that the infinite exists. Schrecker has stated Malebranche's position succinctly: "For Malebranche, as for modern mathematics, infinity is therefore inherent in continuity."[6] Mathematical continuity, we recall from the first chapter, is an idea that is not exhausted through totally logical axioms (pure analysis) that result in tautology nor derived from sensory experience through induction. Rather it is the mathematician's faith in the principle of recurrence, which is necessarily assumed in order to establish mathematical laws. Malebranche was surely right to see, as Descartes did not (in stating that unending divisibility was only indefinite), that there is more than pure privation involved in mathematical infinity. Nonetheless, as related to the principle of recurrence, infinity remains only assumptive for mathematical induction. It 'exists' because it would be impossible to do mathematics were it not assumed to exist. It is therefore established as a condition of thought. This was Malebranche's epistemic meaning when he claimed that the mind has a union with infinity, that the mind perceives it "immediately and directly,"[7] or that "the general idea of infinity is inseparable from the mind."[8]

The infinity grounded in mathematical induction was a conceivable infinity. Conceiving, to reiterate, was the mode of knowing appropriate to mathematical truths and their univocal order. As such it described the operation by which one grasped the possible conditions of thinking about infinite reality, but it did not describe infinite reality itself. In other words, the conceivability of truths was necessary but not sufficient for the claims of metaphysics. In order to ground God's positive infinity as something extending beyond His mere possibility, Malebranche was compelled to rely upon comprehension as the proper mode of knowing. Thus comprehension intuits ideas as real beings ontologically. Comprehension intuits by "simple view" the soul as existing and as finite, and comprehension intuits God (also "by simple view") and His positive infinity as the ontological antipode of man's finitude. When speaking then of the ontological relation between finite man and infinite God, Malebranche argued that its essential and identifying characteristic was the impossibility of continuity. The distance between the infinite and the finite, he wrote, is an infinite distance, which he interpreted to mean that there can be no relation at all.[9] "It is a common notion that between the finite and the infinite there is no relation at all. Everything rests on this indisputable principle."[10] The world is not worthy of God, he stated elsewhere, because "it does not even have any proportion with God,"[11] because of the qualitative separation of the finite from the infinite. A third expression Malebranche used frequently to express the same idea was that "nothing finite contains the infinite."[12] The denial of continuity evident in these phrases was intended to stress the absolute metaphysical gulf between God, the infinite metaphysical reality that is not communicated, and man, whose finitude comprises his chief ontological characteristic. The finite to infinite scale could not be mathematical but was purely ontological, based not on the scale of naturally increasing magnitude from *unité* to infinity but on the polarity of Being and non-being.[13] Relative to God, man remains 'nothing'; relative to man, God remains "hidden" and absolute.[14] Malebranche thus used the archetype of 'number' and its assumed continuity, which is conceived, to establish infinity as necessary to thought but then shifted to a central assumption of 'substance' for a conception of positive infinity sufficient for descriptive metaphysics. This infinity could not be totally comprehended but was established by means of comprehension and intuited directly as existing in its positive features—infinite perfection, wisdom, mercy, power, and goodness. "Or to speak more clearly . . . one can see the infinite only in itself."[15]

This shift in models is equally discernible in Malebranche's treatment of the concept of necessity. In his challenge to scholastic thought, he denied the cognitive value of scholastic demonstrations that utilized syllogistic form to elicit logical necessity between premises and conclusions.[16] Rather, necessity meant the exact, clear and distinct relations between ideas based on 'number'. Mathematical necessity was the referent in his theory of the truths of magnitude, the foundation of universal science. "Those who know perfectly the relations of numbers and figures, or rather the art of making *necessary comparisons* in order to know relations, have a kind of universal science, and a very secure means of discovering with evidence and certitude everything that does not pass beyond the ordinary limits of the mind."[17] The necessary comparisons are those of equality and inequality,[18] and comparing exactly the relations of inequality rests on *unité* as earlier indicated. Further, these necessary comparisons were perceived by the mind as it received the simple relations between numbers (or ratios), as it made judgments (perceptions of two or more simple relations), and as it reasoned (comparisons of two or more judgments).[19] Necessity in comparisons could only mean necessity between relations or, in logical expression, between propositions, not between terms generically conceived, nor between the statements of a syllogism framed of sentences constructed of generic terms. Reasoning with evidence connoted this sense of necessity.[20] This did not transform necessity into a purely analytical concept. Just as the notion of infinity in mathematics is derived necessarily from mathematical induction and its implied continuity and cannot as a result be reduced to a purely analytical description, the result of which is tautology, so it is with necessity, as Malebranche recognized. The possibility of discovering new truths required that necessity be related to the mathematical order of both *unité* and infinity, to the "natural order" of ideas: "It [arithmetic] then teaches how to make . . . the proper calculations to deduce these relations, one from the other, and to discover the relations of magnitude that can be useful by means of those that are known."[21] Deduction means following the necessity in the calculations of mathematics, and necessity serves a purely epistemic function in this conception by helping the mind apprehend the relations through which it can understand things in the world.

Again, however, having established necessity as a condition for knowing truths, the relations between ideas, Malebranche broadened and shifted its meaning to include the necessity between truth that is relational and being that is generic. Thus, "it is absolutely *necessary* that all there is in the world be either a being or a manner of being."[22] The necessity here is ontological. As we saw earlier, it is part of God's nature to have His existence expressed necessarily in the idea we have of Him, just as it is part of His nature that what He wills should necessarily come to pass and that, accordingly, all creation and all causation can be traced necessarily to His Being. The intrinsic necessity of Being expresses itself in thought and unfolds itself in the external world of experience. And necessity in Being is based on 'substance' not 'number'.

The ambiguity in Malebranche's concept of being echoed the ambiguities in his descriptions of infinity and necessity. Consistent with his attack on scholastic logic and the scholastic reliance on demonstrative necessity, he held firmly to the proposition that man cannot know the true nature of particular things or beings as the scholastics claimed. Definitions of things, he agreed, ought to explain their nature, but only if the nature of a thing was considered in its complete generality, not with reference to its particular and sensate manifestations. The only useful portions of traditional thought were the completely general terms such as being-in-general or cause-in-general. All the other little beings or the little causes were specious.[23] Yet even being was not the grandfather of all categories, the substance of substances, but the hypostatized order of relations through which everything in the world that could be known was known. Being, otherwise stated, was purely relational. This is clearly indicated in Malebranche's insistence on considering the essence of matter as extension and all differentiations in extension as simply and completely matters of degree, "of more and less." The essence of matter is captured totally by the relations of magnitude, and because the essence of matter is its intelligibility, intelligibility is the relational and real order to which all beings belong. As has been indicated, this was an order described after the model of 'number'. This order constituted God's substance insofar as it is representative of things in the world. To grasp the relations of intelligible extension was the objective of geometers and mathematicians and, accordingly, the chief goal of all science. One can know the real order, mathematics hypostatized, not things themselves: "I deny that one knows *clearly* the nature of the things one can *count*."[24]

Moreover, the real ideas constituting intelligible order were clearly seen as the models of all things: "Omnipotence is included in the idea of the infinitely perfect Being, [which] as a consequence wills and produces beings whose ideas or models are included in its essence."[25] Because ideas are eternal truths and the models of all things, they determine the order of all possible worlds and are the conditions of possibility itself. As Schrecker writes, "Our science, therefore, manifests the world only as it is possible."[26] As a relational concept then, being describes possibility not actuality, and the possible is converted into the metaphysically real. Indeed, Malebranche ultimately denied that we can know philosophically either soul or matter; all we know are possibilities—the necessary relations that are the models or conditions for understanding mind or body. Because its substantial reality is manifest in the hypostatization of mathematical relations, being can provide no extrasystemic reference to existents outside its own relations. Consequently, reality must either be totally contained within God, and hence we see all things in Him, or it must be completely unintelligible, and therefore not reality and not existent. Everything is God or nothing is. Implied here is that everything in experience must be real in the same fashion as are the relations of magnitude: "Only nothingness is despicable, for all reality merits esteem" equally.[27] From this conception, the charge of Spinozism, often leveled against Malebranche, appears well founded.[28] Reliance on 'number' as an archetype for metaphysics, which resulted in making the possible real, obviated the distinction between possible reality and actual reality by denying independent criteria for distinguishing possibility from actuality. 'Substance' had provided such criteria with its concept of matter that realized its potency through form. But with mathematics the distinction between form and matter becomes meaningless, and consequently when mathematics is taken as the model for metaphysics, the distinction between reality as actual and reality as possible also falls, as it did for Malebranche.

Yet Malebranche rejected the charge of Spinozism and spent considerable effort in his later years refuting the position that intelligible relations and material relations were mutually inclusive metaphysically. As Iorio records, despite Malebranche's claim that matter could not be known with certitude philosophically, he did hold to the probability of matter's real existence as a philosophical contention and not simply for religious reasons.[29] He also maintained the truths of perfection as well as those of magnitude. And the truths of perfection enabled the classification of qualities in the world into the more traditional generic categories. In other words, he could not accept being as purely relational but felt compelled to argue for its substantive nature as well. Hence God possessed all perfections and indeed was all perfections. From His perfection He established all laws in the universe, granted man his liberty, endowed man with His likeness, and provided an order of grace to complement, fulfill, and sustain the natural order. God's perfections may have been of equal value from the divine standpoint, but from man's perspective they were necessarily and qualitatively distinct although, with equal necessity, unknowable in any exact sense. God's justice and the golden rule were as certain as any mathematical relationship.[30] Consequently, being resided in a tension between models. Either it was purely relational, which led to the conversion of all possible reality to necessity and thus to Spinoza, or it was generic, and the qualitative distinctions in being could be maintained— maintained but ultimately not known.

The tension between the models of 'substance' and 'number' in the concepts of infinity, necessity, and being reveals a more fundamental shift in mental patterns apparent in Malebranche, a shift from a logic of terms to a logic of propositions. Attention is directed here not materially to specific ideas that Malebranche developed and utilized but to the function of those ideas. Malebranche himself did not formulate in any conscious manner a logic of propositions. Nonetheless he did frame specific arguments in such a manner as to reflect the model of propositional logic and did so most significantly in his formulation of the ways in which man knows God. The distinction between the two types of logic needs to be specified.

A logic of terms, which emerges from 'substance' assumes first and foremost affirmation of the subject of a proposition prior to predication. For example, in the universal statement 'all men are rational', the subject 'all men' is affirmed with the copula 'are' prior to the addition of the predicate. 'Rational' serves to differentiate what men are from the multiplicity of possible predicates. This mode of framing statements is derived from the metaphysical basis of 'substance'. Differentiation assumes that proper differentia will be discovered, that the categories will not be meaningless combinations of words. It assumes so because the structure of being reveals to the knowing mind the proper terms of predication. When applied to the idea of God, this assumption is extremely important, because it posits the affirmation of God prior to eliciting predicates appropriate to God as the subject of the proposition. Thus for St. Anselm predication in the ontological argument is simply completing intellectually the ontological affirmation initiated in the subject itself. This is the purport behind stating that there is an ontological reality that imposes itself upon thought or that it is God's nature to be efficacious in forming proper predication in the mind. On this model also, the reverse inference becomes possible: from the predication it is proper and necessary to infer the affirmation of the subject. Intuition of perfection then leads directly to acknowledgment of God's reality as perfection. This is clearly what Malebranche did in his inference from the finite, imperfect mind to the infinite, perfect God; and from the idea of infinite perfection to the reality of an ontologically necessary God.

In contrast to this pattern, a logic of propositions, which is derived implicitly from the archetype of 'number', does not postulate the affirmation of the subject prior to predication. Rather it places the whole relation between subject and predicate in a series of hypothetical relationships and stipulates only that 'if x is related to the subject, then x must be related necessarily to the predicate'. Again, using the example of men and their rationality, the form is 'if x is a man, then x is rational'. There is no affirmation of the propositional subject 'x is a man'; it is only hypothetical or possible. The only affirmation is that if 'x is a man' is true, it is equally and necessarily true that 'x is rational'. If the first possibility is established or affirmed, then the second one must necessarily be affirmed as true.[31] This mode or form of framing propositions is clearly derived from the hypothetical form of mathematical statements that joins two propositions in the same fashion.

The implication of this form in the case of the idea of God is momentous. There is no affirmation of the subject God prior to predication, and indeed predication merely establishes the possible conditions of a consistent idea of God. To consider the possible conditions of God is to describe the ideas that must necessarily relate to His idea, with the implication that no extrasystemic reference and hence no 'existence' apart from the relations themselves can be attributed to the subject. God's existence then becomes a prelogical question, one that must be answered totally apart from the canons of univocal thought, since thought indicates only what is necessary to itself. The form of the universal statement as applied to God is: 'if x is God, then x must also be infinite, perfect, omnipotent'. God's existence and reality in this form are purely hypothetical. The lack of any reference outside the relations of logic carries also the futher implication that meaningful statements about God are reducible to either self-reference or self-contradiction, perforce of the laws of identity, noncontradiction, and excluded middle—the laws that underscore a logic of propositions.[32]

The implications of this form reside fully in Malebranche, and it is instructive to note how. In the *Entretiens sur la métaphysique* he wrote that God has within Himself all ideas, that "He includes, therefore, in his wisdom all speculative and practical truths."[33] We must bear in mind that the distinction between speculative and practical truths is a distinction from the perspective of man not of God, in Whom all ideas are of equal value, exactitude, and necessity. If there is a God (that is, if x is God), then He contains all truths (then x possesses all truths). A moment's reflection will elicit the difficulty here. If x is God, then x contains all truths. If x contains all truths, then x contains truths T_1, T_2, T_3 . . . T_n (letting T_n be infinity). But it is also a truth (a real relation) that 'if x is God, then x contains T_1 . . . T_n', and *this* truth is not on the scale of truths designated by T_1 . . . T_n. If it is added to the scale of truths as T_x, then the new relation is written as follows: 'if x is God, then x contains all truths, T_1, T_2 . . . T_x . . . T_n'. But, again a new relation or truth has been established which is not included within the previous predication. Hence it would appear that a vicious and infinite regress emerges, from which two possibilities result: either the relation between the propositional subject and its predicate is a tautology ('if x is omniscient, then x knows what he knows'); or the result is a logically inconsistent idea of omniscience and thus of God. This development is possible in a logic of terms. If one writes, 'God is truth', or the 'Knower of truth', and all truths are T_1, etc., the same difficulty could be shown. But there is a critical difference because of the different forms. In the logic of terms the affirmation of God prior to predication means that predication itself is an ontological discovery. Contradictions found in predication are thus ontological contradictions and when this is accepted the argument is used to establish the ontological limits of the knowing mind not the denial of God.[34] In the logic of propositions the claim that God as an idea is inconsistent rests on the epistemic primacy of the mind to examine through its own contents the conditions of reality.

It bears repeating that Malebranche himself did not consciously formulate the problem of God's being in the above fashion, but in his reliance on 'number' as the model for truths and for metaphysics, the above pattern functioned in his thinking to obviate the form of 'substance' that had been relied upon for centuries. In this regard it is not unjust to charge that Malebranche's Platonism was extrinsic and accidental to the central core of his thought. Further confirmation of the shift to this mode of describing God is borne out historically by the eighteenth century's formulation of the problem of evil. If x is God, then x must be perfect. If x is perfect, then x must be omniscient, omnipotent, omnibenevolent. If x is all of these, then how can one account for evil? From an intuition of evil, either in the sense of moral wrong or of natural suffering, it is a simple argument in the form of modus tollens to deny the possibility of God. The eighteenth-century quandary was clear. On the one hand evil could be redefined as something that is not really evil, and the result is a theodicy or a deification of nature in pantheism. The difference is that theodicy stresses the transcendence, and pantheism, the immanence of the divine. The other option was atheism, since the possible conditions for God were self-contradictory. Hence the disjunctive sense of reality, the central perception of the vision in God, meant that either everything was God or that nothing was, and the eighteenth century's efforts to come to grips with the question of evil were posed in this form of thought, as Lester Crocker has indicated in his study on moral thought of the Enlightenment.[35]

With these two submerged models informing his writings, the result for Malebranche was a conflict between reason and faith, which despite his efforts to the contrary was never overcome. The starkness of the dichotomy in Malebranche's treatment of reason and faith is indicated by his own words. From the *Recherche*: "Only reason ought to preside in the judgment of all human opinions, which have no relation at all to faith, about which God alone instructs us in an entirely different manner from the way He discloses natural things to us."[36] In the *Entretiens*: "Philosophers, my dear Ariste, are obliged to religion, for only it can lead them out of the difficulties in which they find themselves!"[37] In his penetrating article concerning reason and faith in Malebranche, Albert Decourtray has contended that, although Malebranche acknowledged an ambiguous meaning for both faith and reason ("faith is also as equivocal a term as reason"[38]), his chief tendency was to subordinate faith to reason because of his insistent Cartesianism.[39] This interpretation is not without support from Malebranche's works, but the equivocation that Malebranche acknowledged is neither as limited and terminological as he believed, nor as amenable to such an easy resolution as Decourtray contends. The dilemma is structural and epochal.

The sharp separation of religion and faith from science and reason presented initially by Malebranche in the *Recherche* echoed the separatism of Descartes.[40] For Descartes, and for Malebranche in the above passage, reason was given to man by God to understand nature and the natural order of things. Correct reasoning was carried out only with evidence and rested on the inner light that granted assent to "indisputable demonstrations." No authorities were to be acknowledged in any blind sense; each was to be evaluated according to reason, and both men encouraged their readers to develop a love for new discoveries and new truths that were revealed to reason. In contrast, the mysteries of faith expressed a supernatural order, the order of grace. To be affiliated with this order, one neither had nor needed ideas; one needed simply the gift of God's love as expressed through the church and its historically established canons. One ought to accept the authority of the church and her theologians as the proper guardians of religious truths and mysteries. Indeed, man's purpose was to search for spiritual food or spiritual truth, a search founded on faith that came to man only from "revelation and not from the speculation of clear ideas, mathematics, and numbers."[41] In a word, "to be a believer one must believe blindly, but to be a philosopher one must see clearly."[42]

On this division between faith and reason, faith emerged as intuitive, following the meaning of intuitive outlined earlier in Chapter 2. Its core was the intuitive apprehension of grace through the revelations provided by God, who otherwise remained hidden to man.[43] Conversely, reason was purely self-contained and self-evident. Bound only by the clearness and distinctness of its own relations, apprehension of which was necessary for knowledge of nature, it was grounded on those assumptive principles—for example, correspondence and recurrence—necessary to the relations perceived. Mathematics and religion appeared far apart on this reading: "As for mathematical truths, those that measure magnitudes, numbers, times, movements, all that differs only by more and less, I remain in agreement that faith does not help at all to discover them."[44] In this account, faith spoke to man only through the senses and through the body;[45] through it God's grace "conquered" nature, in a manner of speaking, by means of "a particular assistance."[46] The blindness of faith and its exclusivity from ideas were thus corollaries of the particular revelation of God in history as perceived through man's senses and portrayed in scripture.

But if faith was to grasp intuitively God's working in history, it led necessarily beyond apprehension of particular events to the affirmation of divine truth itself and to the truths of meta-physics, the first and foremost of which was recognition of Being and God as universal. In fact, as one scholar has re-marked, religion was so intimately united with metaphysics that Malebranche maintained their virtual identification.[47] He frequently declared that the "mind's attention" was turned necessarily toward God, the only master, who instructs "by the manifestation of His substance."[48] And the manifestation of His substance was not particular but general; His universal being in its manifest totality was "the nature of ideas, and the goodness, the generality, the incomprehensible wisdom of di-vine Providence."[49] In this vein Malebranche even ventured so far as to say that "God never performs miracles"[50] and could be considered only as acting through universal laws according to His universal reason. Just as faith led man to God through the senses, so too did it lead him to grasp intuitively through thought these metaphysical truths. "It [faith] guides me and sustains me in the search for the truths that have some relation to God, as those of metaphysics."[51] The "application of the mind to God,"[52] which affirmed God's existence and His ne-cessity, was inclusive with faith. One submitted himself "of good faith" to his inner convictions in obedience to the inner light of meditations, which was the "voice of our common Mas-ter."[53] In this sense knowledge and faith grew to merge into a single act—apprehension of Being and its universal truths. "To know God is to know truth, or know things according to the truth."[54] Thus when Malebranche described knowledge as the apprehension of relations or truths of mathematics, he con-sidered it to be at least partial knowledge of God's being, His reason. Such relations had to be real because thought, never distinct from the inner light of faith, always affirmed Being.[55] "We are never without thinking of Being."[56] The priority is ontological; faith and thought are concomitants in the affir-mation of that ontological priority. Indeed, one could never conceive of thought without Being, although Being without thought is not only conceivable but necessary.[57]

Malebranche's affinity with the assumptions of 'substance' is apparent in this treatment of reason and faith and is confirmed in his citations of both Augustine and Aquinas. He cited Augustine for support of the immediacy with which God spoke to the mind through inner light: "I believe *that God touches our mind by his essence*; I add, *immediately and directly*, 'NULLA *interposita creatura*,' as Saint Augustine says."[58] In St. Thomas, Malebranche saw support for his theory that the apprehension of ideas is apprehension of the divine essence as it is representative of things. God's single essence provides for the intelligibility of diverse ideas: "One attributes diverse ideas to Him," because "in His single essence God conceives many notions relating to diverse things."[59] Whereas Descartes had taken the term idea and employed it to designate the contents of man's mind, in contrast to the restricted use of the term in the Middle Ages, Malebranche had used it to connote both the direct objects that the mind apprehends and the essence of God insofar as ideas were contained in God's essence. The upshot is that as long as thought guided by inner light takes Being as its object, then faith is a component of thought and shares in the same intuitions and affirmations as does thought. "Reason . . . is in perfect agreement with the Gospel."[60] With faith and thought considered as intuitive and affirmative, Reason must be hypostatized, and the assumptions of 'substance' must guide one's search for truth.

On this ground Malebranche argued that science always presupposed metaphysics[61] and that to apply one's mind to science was to discover God through ideas. Yet, as Malebranche himself described metaphysics, the clear reference was not to principles that were intuitive and ontological in nature but to the assumptive principles of his epistemology: "By metaphysics . . . I mean . . . the general truths that can serve as principles for the particular sciences."[62] The principles that served to ground the particular sciences were those clear and distinct ideas provided in mathematics and the relations of magnitude which constituted the "universal science."[63] Such principles were only those necessary for construction and proof of mathematical relations and their extrinsic, one-to-one correspondence with matter. As the perception of relations between two or more relations, reason did not affirm anything but was purely self-referential and was concerned with nothing outside its own rules for operation.[64] Included among such "natural knowledge" was the certitude of God's existence, or rather the certitude of the necessary principle that "there is a God." Further, "the certitude of faith also rests on this principle."[65] Faith depends upon the existence of God; the existence of God depends upon reason; reason is mathematical in character and rests on those principles necessary to its own construction: "Knowledge of the universal cause or the existence of a God is absolutely necessary, since even the certitude of faith rests on the knowledge of the existence of a God that reason supplies."[66] Such are the truths that the soul perceives through pure understanding, the truths it knows "by the reflection it makes *on itself*"[67]: thought reflecting not upon Being but upon itself in order to establish Being. Its principles are necessarily assumed, and faith contingent upon such principles is an assumptive faith, the sort of faith the mathematician needs when he assumes infinity, continuity, or mathematical induction.[68]

A dual sense of faith, then, and a dual sense of reason compete with one another in the thought of Malebranche. Their competition is a direct result of the conflict between the submerged conceptual models of 'substance' and 'number'. On the model of 'substance', thought affirms the ontological structure of being, while faith as the concomitant of thought is intuitive. But when thought takes itself as its object, when thinking becomes "exact" as Ortega phrases it,[69] and when its separation from being is complete, then thought is self-referential and faith is assumptive. To infer from a faith that is assumptive to one that is intuitive—from a God that is necessary as an epistemic principle to a God that is ontologically real—is an inference wholly gratuitous and grounded in a shift from one mode of thinking to another, from 'number' to 'substance'. The unresolved key question with Malebranche is whether 'number' or 'substance'—epistemology or ontology—has first priority. His continual reference to God, in both idea and reality, as the first principle of being and knowledge would appear to give the nod to ontology. Yet when answering the question, How does one know this?, Malebranche's priority is reversed. The passage bears a second reading: "Those who know perfectly the relations of numbers and figures, or rather the art of making necessary comparisons in order to know relations, have a kind of universal science and a very secure means of discovering with evidence and certitude everything that does not pass beyond the ordinary limits of the mind."[70] The first principles here are epistemological and embrace the assumptions necessary to promote mathematical reasoning, universal science, and the means for discovering everything of which the mind is ordinarily capable. Thought determined by the generic structures of being; being evaluated by the relational conditions of thought: such was the impasse Malebranche left for his successors.

The irony in Malebranche's formulation of the relation between science and religion dwelt in his desire to distinguish science and religion, reason and faith, in order to gain greater insight and clarity into the truths of each and to attempt their ultimate reunification. Other intellectuals drew much from his distinctions and clarifications but said in effect that once rent, the two could not be resewn, at least not in the cloth of tradition. Fénelon, for instance, feared the Oratorian's subsumption of faith and religion in reason as an attack on the mysteries of faith itself. Less concerned with the mysteries of faith, Bayle applauded the clarifications rendered to science and the subsequent defeat of traditional metaphysics.[71] Indeed, even God as a necessary assumption would fall by the wayside before reason had run its course. Laplace's remark to Napoleon was probably apocryphal but nonetheless accurate. Napoleon had complimented Laplace on his recent book on astronomy but then noted that the author had made no mention of God, to which the eminent scientist replied: "I had no need of this hypothesis."

The deep structures of 'substance' and 'number', then, in Malebranche's thought gave form to the most central dilemma in connection with science and religion in the seventeenth century. The question centered on the relation between epistemology and ontology, on whether or not the new forms of knowledge generated by the revolution in science and the accompanying revolution in thought could lend any support at all to metaphysical truths beyond those principles necessary for their own operations. Malebranche's explicit answer to the question was yes, but as is evident the yes was gratuitous. The assumptions of mathematical recurrence or periodicity, the foundation for reformulated principles of uniformity and economy in nature, and of correspondence, the foundation for the connection between the world of ideas and the world of nature, were both necessary as assumptive principles for thought and for science. The being of God, either as an hypostatization of mathematical order in intelligible extension or as a generic absolute supported by the assumptions of 'substance' was gratuitous to those necessary principles. Gradual acceptance of, and reliance upon, the univocal reasoning of 'number' as the chief intellectual priority meant ultimately that no cognitive sense could be made of Being and 'substance'.

Small wonder Pascal loathed the geometer's god.

Notes

(Unless otherwise noted in the bibliography, all translations from French are the author's.)

Chapter 1

1. While there was certainly not *one* but a variety of scientific methods in the late seventeenth century, it was by then evident that scientific truths would be formulated in mathematical terms and confirmed through experiment and/or exact observation. It is this more general sense of "method" that gained increasing and widespread support.

2. Hazard, *European Mind*, p. 134.

3. Gueroult, *Malebranche*, 1:12.

4. See, for example, White, *Metahistory*, pp. 1–43 and passim. Whereas White elicits the poetic structures of historical imagination of several nineteenth-century figures, the present effort concentrates on the structures of religious and scientific imagination, the 'root metaphors' that gave these structures cohesion, their connection with broader philosophical traditions, and their conflict in Malebranche.

5. For example, Church, *Philosophy of Malebranche*.

6. For example, Rome, *Philosophy of Malebranche*. While Rome's work offers many fine insights into Malebranche's thought, the overall achievement is as labyrinthine as the Oratorian himself.

7. Black, *Models and Metaphors*, pp. 219–43. See also his fine essay, "Metaphors," in the same volume, pp. 25–47.

8. Butterfield, *Modern Science*, p. 7.

9. Cassirer, "Some Remarks," p. 51.

10. Kline, *Mathematics*, p. 14.

11. For the purpose of clarification, single quotation marks will be used to distinguish the models of 'number' and 'substance' from the concepts of number and substance.

12. Ortega y Gasset, *Idea of Principle*, passim.

13. Whitehead, *Science*, pp. 33–34.

14. Cassirer, *Substance*, pp. 4–5.

15. Ortega y Gasset, *Idea of Principle*, pp. 58–62. To elaborate his meaning of the "concept as term," Ortega wielded a bit of mythology that merits paraphrasing. The process of eliciting "mental extracts" limits the meaning of an intuition to its definition, which, once defined, is no longer unlimited, undifferentiated, diffuse. The word Aristotle used to express this idea of concept was "*horos*"; its Latin equivalent was "*terminus*." Both *horos* and *terminus* originally signified the piles of stones, and later markers, that separated fields, delimiting property. The Greeks created a god of boundary markers, Hermes, who also stood at crossroads to differentiate roadways. Since the right road was called 'method' in Greek, Hermes was considered among other things a god of salvation. Now concepts, like boundaries, look in two directions: *ad extra* and *ad intra*. Looking out upon reality they pretend to tell us the veracity of what they see; looking inward they are concerned solely with their own logical exactness. (Today, dispensing with myth, perhaps unfortunately, this is simply cited as the extension and intension of a concept.) This ordering of concepts is the function of Aristotle's logic; it is thus a logic of *terms*, vis-à-vis one of propositions. And the mythical element in this description conveys the sense of value—the mind's right path to salvation, as it were—intrinsic to Aristotle's system.

16. Ibid.

17. Cassirer, *Substance*, p. 6.

18. Ortega y Gasset, *Idea of Principle*, p. 224.

19. Cassirer, *Substance*, pp. 6–7.

20. Aristotle, *Metaphysics*, Bk. Δ, 8, 1017b. Some modern scholars, notably Jan Lukasiewicz (*Aristotle's Syllogistic*), point out that it is a mistake to read a priority of metaphysics into Aristotle, especially as regards his logic, which, although a logic of terms, does not presup-

pose an ontogenesis of their formation; rather Aristotle's syllogistic is purely formal. Thus Lukasiewicz notes, *horos* has two distinct meanings for Aristotle: as an "empty" term of a premise in a formal syllogism; as a definition with "psychological" and/or "metaphysical" content. Aristotle's stress was on the former (Lukasiewicz, *Aristotle's Syllogistic*, pp. 3–4). It is nonetheless correct to say that, for scholastic philosophers of the Middle Ages and for intellectuals of the seventeenth century in general, this distinction was obviated, and Aristotle's logic was understood to rest on metaphysics and 'substance' in the manner suggested. See, for example, Loemker, *Struggle for Synthesis*, pp. 227–28.

21. Randall, *Aristotle*, pp. 110–23.

22. Cassirer, *Substance*, p. 7.

23. Randall, *Aristotle*, p. 110.

24. Copleston, *History of Philosophy*, v. 1, pt. 2:21. Aristotle did not claim that things always existed in extramental reality precisely as they were conceived by the mind. Nonetheless, as Copleston writes, his logic was "an analysis of the thought that thinks reality, that reproduces it conceptually within itself, and . . . makes statements about reality which are verified in an external world."

25. Ortega y Gasset, *Idea of Principle*, p. 112; Lovejoy, *Great Chain of Being*, pp. 57–59. As described here 'substance' bears an affinity to Lovejoy's "great chain of being." The reason for adopting the former as an organizing model instead of Lovejoy's term is that 'substance' stresses the classificatory mode of abstraction that underlies the chain of being, its hierarchical manner of deriving universal terms, and its ontological presuppositions. It thus gives us a sharper focus on traditional thought and leads to a more thorough comprehension of the innovations of the seventeenth century which emerge from mathematics than does Lovejoy's concept.

26. Popkin, *Scepticism*, chapters 1–3.

27. Ortega y Gasset, *Idea of Principle*, p. 125 and passim; Dijksterhuis, *Mechanization*, p. 70.

28. Francis Bacon, cited in McRae, "Unity of the Sciences," pp. 30–31.

29. Poincaré, *Foundations of Science*, pp. 210–22.

30. From this description it would seem that Poincaré is in accord with Kant that discoveries in mathematics are in the order of synthetic *a priori* judgments. However, Poincaré is somewhat ambivalent on this point. See Waismann, *Mathematical Thinking*, p. 89ff.

31. Descartes, *Philosophical Works*, 1:91.

32. Ibid., 1:209.

33. Dantzig, *Number*, pp. 59, 98.

34. Poincaré, *Foundations of Science*, p. 44.

35. For example, whole numbers and fractions are species of the class 'rational'; rational and irrational numbers belong to the class 'real', and so forth. The 'meaning' of a number, however, is not contingent upon this classification.

36. My chief interest here is not in a technical mastery of the issues involved in mathematics, philosophy of mathematics, or logic as developed by Dedekind, Cantor, Frege, Peano, Whitehead, Russell, Poincaré, and other nineteenth- and twentieth-century logicians, mathematicians, and philosophers whose work resulted in the clarification and refinement of the number idea. Rather, it is in some of the features of mathematics and number, revealed by these investigations, that can serve as clues to understanding both the attraction and the implications that mathematics had for Descartes, Malebranche, and other intellectuals of the seventeenth century. Consequently I have relied upon more general discussions of mathematical thought, including the following: Dantzig, *Number* and *Aspects of Science*; Cassirer, *Substance*; Poincaré, *Foundations of Science*; Whitehead, *Mathematics* and *Science and Philosophy*; Bell, *Mathematics*; Struik, *Mathematics*; Bochner, *Mathematics*; Waismann, *Mathematical Thinking*; Russell, *Mathematical Philosophy*; Black, *Mathematics*.

37. Dantzig, *Number*, pp. 7–8.

38. Ibid.

39. Cassirer, *Substance*, p. 48.

40. Dantzig, *Number*, p. 8.

41. Ibid., p. 9.

42. It should be noted that these comments are restricted to real numbers and are not extended to complex or transfinite numbers.

43. Waismann, *Mathematical Thinking*, pp. 25–48.

44. Whitehead, *Science*, p. 35.

45. Ibid., pp. 25–29.

46. Nagel, "'Impossible Numbers'," p. 451ff.

47. Cassirer, *Substance*, p. 39.

48. Bell, *Mathematics*, p. 19.

49. Dantzig, *Number*, p. 77.

Chapter 2

1. Boas, *Scientific Renaissance*, pp. 197–237. In mentioning the history of algebra, it is necessary to distinguish three stages of development: (a) "rhetorical algebra," characterized by the lack of symbols, except insofar as words are used in a symbolic sense—e.g., "the sum is independent of the order of the terms"; (b) "syncopated algebra," a further development of the rhetorical, with some words evolving into symbols—e.g., from "minus" in the middle ages, to the letter "m" superscribed as "m̅", to the modern symbol "−"; (c) "symbolic algebra," in which all the operations and relations of algebra are handled exclusively through the use and manipulations of symbols—e.g., $a+b+c=b+c+a$ is a symbolic expression of the rhetorically stated principle above. See Dantzig, *Number*, pp. 78–92; Burtt, *Metaphysical Foundations*, pp. 41–51.

2. Dijksterhuis, *Mechanization*, p. 404.

3. Maritain, *Dream*, pp. 11–31 and passim.

4. The phrase "incommunicability of the genera" refers to a feature of scholastic and ancient thought. Because they reflected ontological substances that were distinct from one another, the genera shared nothing in common, and hence the proper methods for the study of different genera were contingent upon the genus under examination. For example, it was thought that the genera of arithmetic, marked by discontinuity or number units, and geometry, marked by continuity or extended magnitude, were derived from different sense perceptions, the former from the intuition of the 'number-thing', the latter from the intuition of the 'extension-thing'. Since there was no concrete concept that could be derived from sensory intuition *common* to both continuity and discontinuity, the genera remained "incommunicable." See Ortega y Gasset, *Idea of Principle*, pp. 218–31.

5. *Rules*, 1, *Philosophical Works*, 1:1.

6. *Rules*, 14, ibid., 1:64.

7. *Rules*, 5, ibid., 1:14.

8. *Rules*, 6, ibid., 1:15–16.

9. *Rules*, 3, 6, ibid., 1:7, 16.

10. Descartes' use of "simple essences" or "natures" (the Latin is "*naturas*") was not without ambiguity. At times he retained the generic signification, as when the term was applied to "things" either "spiritual or corporeal or at once spiritual and corporeal" (*Rules*, 7 and 12, ibid., 1:27 and 41 respectively). But it is equally evident that he

consciously sought to transform "essence" into relation on the model of 'number' in his discussion of "essence" as the "primary and simplest proposition" (ibid., 1:17). Implicit here is a shift from the logic of terms, generically formed on the model of 'substance' to one of propositions, based on mathematics. As we shall see later, Malebranche furthered this shift.

11. *Rules*, 6, ibid., 1:15–18.

12. Ibid.

13. *Rules*, 14, ibid., 1:55.

14. Ibid., 1:56, 63–64. A key term in Descartes' understanding of "comparison" was the Latin "*aequalitas*," which Haldane and Ross translated as "uniformity": "The chief part of our human industry consists in merely so transmuting these ratios as to show clearly a uniformity between the matter sought for and something else already known. . . . We must mark that nothing can be reduced to this uniformity, save that which admits of a greater and a less, and that all such matter is included under the term magnitude." This is a mistranslation, since what Descartes had in mind was an equation that involved at least one unknown and could, in turn, be related by the equals sign to something else known. *Aequalitas* thus referred to equality, as noted in the French translation of Jacques Brunschwig, who translates the word as "*égalité*." *Oeuvres philosophiques*, 1:169.

15. *Règles*, 14, *Oeuvres philosophiques*, 1:182. The French rendition is much clearer than the English of Haldane and Ross, primarily because of the dual sense of *unité*, an ambiguity that, as we shall see, was of critical significance for Malebranche.

16. Robinet, "Philosophie malebranchiste," pp. 206–7.

17. In Rule 7 Descartes states that the "movement of thought" must be "continuous and nowhere interrupted." The modern phrasing for this characteristic of mathematical abstraction is "everywhere dense." *Philosophical Works*, 1:19.

18. In Rule 3 Descartes used the phrase "*intuitus scilicet et inductio*." Haldane and Ross translated *inductio* as "induction," but clearly Descartes here meant *deduction* because he was describing the two mental operations. This is confirmed in Rules 11 and 12 where he wrote of the two mental operations as intuition and deduction, not intuition and induction.

19. *Rules*, 7, ibid., 1:19–22.

20. *Oeuvres philosophiques*, 1:230.

21. See Gilson's comment that Descartes was always moving in

"wider concentric circles" in his efforts to seek a more general method. Gilson, *Philosophical Experience*, p. 135.

22. Cited in McRae, "Unity of the Sciences," p. 37.

23. Malebranche will later parallel this construction with a description of order progressing from simple relations to judgments to reasoning.

24. Balz, *Descartes*, p. 338.

25. *Oeuvres*, 2:597.

26. Dantzig, *Number*, p. 179.

27. Ibid., pp. 172–80.

28. This axiom states: "It is possible to assign to any point on a line a unique real number, and, conversely, any real number can be represented in a unique manner by a point on a line." Ibid.

29. *Meditations*, 6, *Philosophical Works*, 1:186.

30. Whitehead, *Science*, p. 28.

31. Balz, *Descartes*, p. 338: "Everything turns upon the question as to how specific correlations between essences and existents can be established."

32. Gewirth, "Experience," p. 188.

33. E. J. Ashworth, "Descartes' Theory of Clear and Distinct Ideas," in Butler, *Cartesian Studies*, p. 91; also Kenny, *Descartes*, p. 96.

34. Ashworth, "Descartes' Theory," p. 91. See *Meditations*, 5, *Philosophical Works*, 1:185.

35. "Response to Third Objections," ibid., 2:67–68.

36. "Reply to Second Objections," ibid., 2:52.

37. Brunschvicg, "Mathématique et métaphysique," p. 290.

38. Enriques, *Development of Logic*, p. 68.

39. Salmon, "Mathematical Roots," pp. 168–69; Gibson, *Philosophy of Descartes*, p. 154; also, *Principles*, pt. 1, 45, *Philosophical Works*, 1:237.

40. *Rules*, 3, ibid., 1:8.

41. Brunschvicg, *Écrits philosophiques*, pp. 55–56.

42. Randall, *Career of Philosophy*, p. 371: "The characteristic problem of modern philosophy has been the conflict of new knowledge with traditional thought, and the attempt to find some adjustment between them. . . . Descartes . . . started modern philosophy."

43. *Rules*, 12, *Philosophical Works*, 1:41.

44. *Philosophical Letters*, p. 138 (italics added).

45. These categories are repeated in the *Meditations*, 3, *Philosophical Works*, 1:165.

46. *Principles*, pt. 1, 21, ibid., 1:227.

47. *Principles*, pt. 1, 51, ibid., 1:239.

48. Ibid.

49. "Reply to Second Objections," ibid., 2:53.

50. This claim was ambiguous; see the distinction between "indefinite" and "infinite" as applies to God, below, pp. 43–44.

51. Brunschvicg, "Mathématique et métaphysique," p. 299.

52. "Reply to Second Objections," *Philosophical Works*, 2:34, 56. Aristotle's analysis of cause into four categories assumed this creationist import; if causing meant bringing into existence some thing or portion of being, then the obvious questions were those of what, how, and why was this accomplished. (When and where were accidental to substance and hence to its causation.) The 'what' was thus the material cause; the 'how' comprised agency (efficient cause) and plan (formal cause); the 'why', purpose (final cause).

53. Brunschvicg, "Mathématique et métaphysique," p. 300; Gilson, *Spirit of Medieval Philosophy*, p. 86.

54. *Principles*, pt. 2, 11, *Philosophical Works*, 1:259.

55. "Reply to Second Objections," ibid., 2:56; Dijksterhuis, *Mechanization*, p. 409–10.

56. "Reply to Second Objections," *Philosophical Works*, 2:57. This formulation too was not without its ambiguities, as will be seen with Malebranche.

57. This is a corollary of the incommunicability of substances. Because they were incommunicable, they could only stand in juxtaposition to each other, not in substantial union.

58. Brunschvicg, "Mathématique et métaphysique," pp. 298–99.

59. *Philosophical Letters*, pp. 137–38.

60. Brunschvicg, "Mathématique et métaphysique," pp. 298–99.

61. Conforming to standard scholarly practice, references to the *cogito*, in italics and without quotation marks, mean the dictum as a whole, while "Cogito" refers to only the first part of it, "I think."

62. *Discourse*, 4, *Philosophical Works*, 1:101.

63. *Rules*, 12, ibid., 1:43.

64. Cited in Brunschvicg, "Mathématique et métaphysique," p. 311.

65. A more thoroughly philosophical formulation of this description is given by von Leyden, *Seventeenth-Century Metaphysics*, pp. 107–28. He interprets the *cogito* as expressing the distinction between the act and the content of self-awareness. Descartes knows himself to

be thinking only when thinking is the object of his thought, i.e., when the act of self-awareness is objectified and expressed as a mental content. The two senses of "I" are: (a) as object, "me"; and (b) as subject, "I," or ego. There is a considerable body of philosophical literature offering analyses of the *cogito* as a statement of, for example, performance, inference, existential affirmation, or syllogistic reasoning. For an introduction to the debate, the collection of articles by Doney is excellent. See especially the articles by Hintikka, Williams, Ayer, and Malcom. Also Doney provides a good bibliography of further works in English on the topic. By contrast to these analyses, my intention is not to develop an in-depth examination of the *cogito* per se but rather to indicate certain features in the *cogito* that are reflective of traditional thinking and others that indicate departure from tradition.

66. *Discourse*, 4, *Philosophical Works*, 1:101.

67. *Meditations*, 3, ibid., 1:163.

68. Brunschvicg, "Mathématique et métaphysique," pp. 302–3.

69. *Meditations*, 5, *Philosophical Works*, 1:181.

70. Ibid.

71. *Philosophical Letters*, pp. 156–58.

72. Ibid.

73. *Meditations*, 4, *Philosophical Works*, 1:172.

74. Brunschvicg, *Écrits philosophiques*, p. 58.

75. *Oeuvres philosophiques*, 1:537–38.

76. Brunschvicg, "Mathématique et métaphysique," pp. 304–5.

77. Watson, *Downfall of Cartesianism*, passim. Watson's valuable study places emphasis on the conflicts between epistemological and ontological principles as the chief reason for the decline of Cartesianism. This decline was encouraged significantly by the academic and sceptic, Canon Foucher, who brought these conflicts into sharp focus in his polemics against Malebranche, Desgabets, Louis de la Forge, Rohault, Régis, and other Cartesians. Part of the present thesis, as we shall see more clearly with Malebranche, is that the source of these conflicts lay in the tensions between two tendencies of abstract thinking, tendencies connoted by the models of 'substance' and 'number'.

78. *Philosophical Letters*, p. 73.

79. Koyré, *Closed World*, pp. 110–24.

80. *Philosophical Letters*, p. 242.

81. Ibid., p. 132.

82. Ibid., p. 254.

83. See R. G. Collingwood's lucid description of the distinction between "assumptive" and "intuitive" in regard to religious expression in *Speculum Mentis*, pp. 132–35.

Chapter 3

1. The best biographical accounts of Malebranche's intellectual development are Gouhier, *Vocation de Malebranche*, and Robinet, *Système et existence*.

2. The phrase is from Bracken, "Problems of Substance," p. 129.

3. Schrecker, "Malebranche et mathématiques," pp. 33–40; "Arnauld, Malebranche, Prestet," pp. 82–90; "Parallélisme," pp. 215–52; Robinet, "Philosophie malebranchiste," pp. 205–54; "Le groupe malebranchiste," pp. 287–308; "Jean Prestet," pp. 95–104; "La vocation académicienne," pp. 1–18.

4. Schrecker, "Malebranche et mathématiques," p. 34.

5. Malebranche, *Recherche*, *Oeuvres*, 1:19.

6. *Recherche*, *Oeuvres*, 2:305, 424.

7. *Entretiens*, *Oeuvres*, 12:58.

8. *Recherche*, *Oeuvres*, 2:305.

9. Ibid., 2:305–6; André, *Vie du R. P. Malebranche*, p. 38.

10. See Descartes, *Rules*, 5, *Philosophical Works*, 1:14.

11. *Oeuvres*, 19:797.

12. *Recherche*, *Oeuvres*, 2:295.

13. Ibid., 2:321.

14. Ibid., 2:302, 349.

15. Ibid., 1:187.

16. Ibid., 2:424.

17. Although not in complete accord about Malebranche's primary intention in writing the *Recherche*, many scholars agree that one of his principal goals was to show that the unreliability of the senses led inevitably to the complete subjectivity of sensation and concomitantly that the objectivity of knowledge could be found only in "pure understanding." See Dolson, "Idealism of Malebranche," pp. 389–92; Luce, *Berkeley and Malebranche*, p. 44; Connell, *Vision in God*, p. 48.

18. Rome, *Philosophy of Malebranche*, pp. 27–28.

19. *Recherche*, *Oeuvres*, 2:245.

20. Ibid., 2:246.

21. Ibid., 1:55.

22. Ibid., 2:296.

23. Ibid.

24. Ibid., 2:296–97 (italics added).

25. Luce, *Berkeley and Malebranche*, p. 16; Rome, *Philosophy of Malebranche*, pp. 7–9.

26. In her "Introduction" to the *Recherche*, Geneviève Rodis-Lewis writes that Malebranche was in contact with Clerselier, executor of Descartes' papers, and that in all probability he had read the *Rules* in manuscript. *Oeuvres*, 1:xxv. It was Clerselier's practice to circulate Descartes' unpublished manuscripts among interested and close friends. "Malebranche must certainly have seen them [*Rules*]." Beck, *Method of Descartes*, pp. 1–2.

27. *Rules*, 5, *Philosophical Works*, 1:14.

28. *Rules*, 14, ibid., 1:64. See also editor's notes nos. 140, 144, 146, 151 for further evidence of the affinity of Malebranche's method with Descartes' *Rules*. *Recherche*, *Oeuvres*, 2:548–49.

29. *Recherche*, *Oeuvres*, 2:297.

30. Ibid., 2:298.

31. Ibid., 2:298–99.

32. Gouhier, *Vocation de Malebranche*, pp. 63–64.

33. Brunschvicg, *Les étapes*, p. 132.

34. Above, page 27.

35. Brunschvicg, *Les étapes*, p. 132.

36. *Recherche*, *Oeuvres*, 2:274.

37. Ibid.

38. Ibid., 2:289.

39. Ibid., 2:89–90; Robinet, "Philosophie malebranchiste," pp. 208–10.

40. *Recherche*, *Oeuvres*, 2:89–90.

41. Ibid., 1:63.

42. Ibid.

43. *Entretiens*, *Oeuvres*, 12:190–91.

44. *Recherche*, *Oeuvres*, 2:286–87; *Méditations chrétiennes*, *Oeuvres*, 10:38–39.

45. *Recherche*, *Oeuvres*, 2:286–87.

46. Ibid.

47. Ibid., 1:475.

48. Ibid., 2:384.

49. Ibid., 2:384–85.
50. Ibid., 2:288.
51. Robinet, "Philosophie malebranchiste," p. 214.
52. *Recherche*, *Oeuvres*, 2:287–88.
53. Ibid., 2:373–74.
54. *Réponse à la troisieme lettre de Arnauld*, *Oeuvres*, 9:926.
55. *Recherche*, *Oeuvres*, 2:288.
56. The use of 'term' in these and similar passages is not to be confused with 'term' described according to the model of 'substance' in Chapter 1. Here it is evident that 'term' refers to mathematical concepts—numbers, letters, functions, symbols—not generic classes.
57. *Recherche*, *Oeuvres*, 2:288–89.
58. Robinet, "Philosophie malebranchiste," pp. 220–26.
59. *Recherche*, *Oeuvres*, 2:289.
60. Ibid., first edition (1674).
61. Ibid., 1:478.
62. Cited in Robinet, "Philosophie malebranchiste," pp. 216, 221. Robinet argues that Prestet's *Éléments des mathématiques* provides evidence for Malebranche's theory of mathematics because Prestet wrote the *Éléments* under Malebranche's direct tutelage. See also, "Jean Prestet," pp. 95–104.
63. *Recherche*, *Oeuvres*, 2:288.
64. Ibid., 1:478–79.
65. In Robinet, "Philosophie malebranchiste," pp. 216, 221.
66. Ibid., p. 222.
67. Above, page 61.
68. *Recherche*, *Oeuvres*, 2:290, 1712 edition.
69. Robinet, "Philosophie malebranchiste," p. 222.
70. *Recherche*, *Oeuvres*, 2:293, 1712 edition.
71. Robinet, "Philosophie malebranchiste," p. 223.
72. Above, page 54.
73. *Recherche*, *Oeuvres*, 1:173, 445; *Éclaircissements*, 1, 8, 11, *Oeuvres*, 3:35, 71, 170; *Traité de nature*, *Oeuvres*, 5:34.
74. *Règles*, 14, *Oeuvres philosophiques*, 1:182.
75. *Recherche*, *Oeuvres*, 2:291.
76. Ibid., 2:289–90.
77. Ibid.
78. *Traité de nature*, *Oeuvres*, 5:80.
79. Robinet, "Le groupe malebranchiste," pp. 287–91; Hankins, "Influence of Malebranche," pp. 193–210.

80. *Recherche, Oeuvres*, 2:35.
81. Ibid., 1:54–55.
82. *Entretiens, Oeuvres*, 12:68.
83. *Recherche, Oeuvres*, 2:287.
84. Ibid., 2:292.
85. Ibid., 2:251.
86. Schrecker, "Malebranche et mathématiques," p. 34; Iorio, "Intelligible Extension," p. 145. Iorio writes that, for Malebranche, science "is concerned with intelligible truths and scientific knowledge is the perception of and attention to these truths."

Chapter 4

1. *Éclaircissements*, 3, *Oeuvres*, 3:44.
2. Arnauld, *Vraies et des fausses idées, Oeuvres philosophiques*, pp. 36–38; *Recherche, Oeuvres*, 1:41–42, 413–14.
3. For a description of this dispute, see: Church, *Philosophy of Malebranche*, chapters 6–8; Loemker, "Leibniz's Discourse," pp. 449–66; Schrecker, "Arnauld, Malebranche, Prestet," pp. 82–90; Laird, "Arnauld's Realism," pp. 176–79; Laird, "Malebranche," pp. 32–47; Lovejoy, "'Representative Ideas'," pp. 449–61; Lovejoy, "Reply to Professor Laird," pp. 180–81; Lewis, "L'intervention de Nicole," pp. 483–507.
4. *Recherche, Oeuvres*, 1:444, first edition.
5. "Second lettre de Malebranche," *Oeuvres*, 9:1002; Augustine, *Free Choice of the Will*, pp. 63–67; Connell, *Vision in God*, pp. 150–51.
6. *Recherche, Oeuvres*, 1:478.
7. *Philosophe chrétien, Oeuvres*, 15:50.
8. *Entretiens, Oeuvres*, 12:86.
9. *Oeuvres*, 19:911.
10. *Réponse à la troisieme lettre de Arnauld, Oeuvres*, 9:949.
11. *Oeuvres*, 19:887.
12. *Recherche, Oeuvres*, 1:41.
13. Ibid., 1:42.
14. Ibid., 1:49–50.
15. Schrecker, "Parallélisme," p. 224.
16. *Recherche, Oeuvres*, 1:49–50.
17. Randall, *Career of Philosophy*, p. 428.

18. Foucher, *Critique*, pp. 117–18.

19. The positions Malebranche refutes are: (1) that ideas originate in material objects; (2) that souls have the power to produce them upon external stimulation; (3) that they are innate in the soul; (4) that the soul considers its own modifications to discover things in the world. *Recherche*, *Oeuvres*, 1:418–34. For a thorough discussion of these refutations, Connell, *Vision in God*, pp. 160–205, is excellent. See also Church, *Philosophy of Malebranche*, pp. 120–24; and Rome, *Philosophy of Malebranche*, pp. 74–116.

20. *Éclaircissements*, 10, *Oeuvres*, 3:148.

21. *Entretiens*, *Oeuvres*, 12:33.

22. *Éclaircissements*, 10, *Oeuvres*, 3:148.

23. Ibid., 3:151.

24. *Entretiens*, *Oeuvres*, 12:42–43, 51.

25. *Éclaircissements*, 10, *Oeuvres*, 3:153.

26. This position is ambiguous; see Chapter 7.

27. *Entretiens*, *Oeuvres*, 12:56–57.

28. Ibid., 12:58.

29. Schrecker, "Parallélisme," p. 231.

30. *Méditations chrétiennes*, *Oeuvres*, 10:99.

31. *Entretiens*, *Oeuvres*, 12:60.

32. Brunschvicg, *Les étapes*, pp. 134–38.

33. Laporte, *Étude d'histoire*, pp. 164, 174.

34. Iorio, "Intelligible Extension," p. 193.

35. Schrecker, "Malebranche et mathématiques," p. 38; *Réponse à la troisieme lettre de Arnauld*, *Oeuvres*, 9:930.

36. Ibid.

37. Ibid., 9:931.

38. *Traité de morale*, *Oeuvres*, 11:20–21.

39. *Entretiens*, *Oeuvres*, 12:64.

40. Ibid., 12:51–52.

41. Ibid.

42. Iorio, "Intelligible Extension," p. 133.

43. Watson, *Downfall of Cartesianism*, p. 33.

44. Aquinas, *Summa Theologiae*, 2:108.

45. Ibid., 1:94. The ontological status of the form was the nub of the medieval argument over universals. Leff, *Medieval Thought*, pp. 104–14; Knowles, *Evolution of Medieval Thought*, pp. 107–15.

46. Aquinas, *Disputed Questions*, in McKeon, *Medieval Philosophers*, 2:165.

47. The theory of adequation was not without its earlier critics. Among others William of Ockham challenged the legitimacy of eliciting general concepts from sensations, while Montaigne later attacked both sensation as a foundation for knowledge and the truth value of general concepts based on sensation. Earlier criticisms of the 'substance' model, however, lacked the grounding in mathematics and 'number' that proved so pivotal in the seventeenth century. See Leff, *Medieval Thought*, pp. 279–94, and Popkin, *Scepticism*, chapter 3.

48. Foucher, *Critique*, pp. 50–52.

49. Above, page 36.

50. Connell, *Vision in God*, p. 36.

51. *Recherche*, *Oeuvres*, 1:215, 141–42.

52. Ibid., 1:121.

53. Ibid., 1:216.

54. *Pièces jointes*, *Oeuvres*, 17:501.

55. *Recherche*, *Oeuvres*, 1:217–18.

56. *Éclaircissements*, 10, *Oeuvres*, 3:153.

57. *Entretiens*, *Oeuvres*, 12:54–55.

58. Brunschvicg, *Les étapes*, p. 132.

59. *Éclaircissements*, 10, *Oeuvres*, 3:153.

60. *Réponse à la troisieme lettre de Arnauld*, *Oeuvres*, 9:929.

61. *Oeuvres*, 19:886.

62. Ibid., 19:910.

63. Iorio, "Intelligible Extension," p. 190.

64. *Entretiens*, *Oeuvres*, 12:19–20.

65. *Recherche*, *Oeuvres*, 2:99–102.

66. Schrecker, "Malebranche et mathématiques," p. 39; "Parallélisme," p. 247.

67. *Recherche*, *Oeuvres*, 2:99–102.

68. Ibid., 1:441.

69. Schrecker, "Parallélisme," p. 247.

70. Cassirer, "Some Remarks," p. 52.

Chapter 5

1. Robinet, "Philosophie malebranchiste," pp. 229–30.

2. Hankins, "Influence of Malebranche," passim; Robinet, "Le groupe malebranchiste," passim.

3. Robinet, "La vocation académicienne," pp. 1–9.

4. Gouhier, *Vocation de Malebranche*, passim.

5. *Traité de nature*, *Oeuvres*, 5:7.

6. Hazard, *European Mind*, pp. 133–38.

7. *Recherche*, *Oeuvres*, 1:1.

8. Ibid., 1:40–48.

9. *Éclaircissements*, 12, *Oeuvres*, 3:174.

10. Ibid.

11. Connell, *Vision in God*, p. 175.

12. *Recherche*, *Oeuvres*, 1:190.

13. *Éclaircissements*, 2, *Oeuvres*, 3:39–41.

14. *Entretiens*, *Oeuvres*, 12:33.

15. Ibid., 12:34.

16. Ibid., 12:74.

17. *Recherche*, *Oeuvres*, 1:381–83.

18. Ibid., 1:381, 459.

19. *Prémotion physique*, *Oeuvres*, 16:40. Here Malebranche wrote that substance is not perishable but modifications are, although when modifications undergo change, so does substance. Nonetheless, the critical point remains that modifications add no new perfection to substance.

20. Connell, *Vision in God*, p. 33.

21. Ibid., *Recherche*, *Oeuvres*, 1:462; *Prémotion physique*, *Oeuvres*, 16:58–59.

22. Above, pages 9–10.

23. Truest here meant simply the most perfect, as when a potter 'trues' his bowl by making it as perfectly round as possible.

24. Collingwood, *Idea of Nature*, pp. 55–57; Lovejoy, *Great Chain of Being*, pp. 24–66.

25. *Recherche*, *Oeuvres*, 2:286.

26. *Traité de morale*, *Oeuvres*, 11:21.

27. For example, Copi, *Introduction to Logic*, pp. 250ff.

28. *Entretiens*, *Oeuvres*, 12:32.

29. *Réponse à la troisieme lettre de Arnauld*, *Oeuvres*, 9:945–47; *Méditations chrétiennes*, *Oeuvres*, 10:37.

30. *Réponse au livre*, *Oeuvres*, 6:163; also, *Oeuvres*, 19:605.

31. Cf. Descartes' notion of a "certain negative idea of nothing," above, page 41.

32. *Éclaircissements*, 12, *Oeuvres*, 3:174.

33. Aristotle, *Metaphysics*, Bk. T, 2, 1003b.

34. *Méditations chrétiennes*, *Oeuvres*, 10:95.

35. *Philosophe chrétien*, *Oeuvres*, 15:5.

36. *Recherche*, *Oeuvres*, 1:456.

37. Collingwood, *Idea of Nature*, p. 57. Elsewhere, Malebranche also denies the theory of emanations, whereby being, perforce of its goodness, overflows into lesser modes of reality and imperfection and finally to non-being (Aristotle's pure potentiality). *Oeuvres*, 19:605.

38. *Entretiens*, *Oeuvres*, 12:190–91.

39. *Philosophe chrétien*, *Oeuvres*, 15:25.

40. *Recherche*, *Oeuvres*, 1:46.

41. *Philosophe chrétien*, *Oeuvres*, 15:25.

42. *Recherche*, *Oeuvres*, 1:20.

43. Ibid., 1:448ff.

44. Ibid., 1:416; *Entretiens*, *Oeuvres*, 12:64.

45. *Entretiens*, *Oeuvres*, 12:65.

46. *Recherche*, *Oeuvres*, 1:55.

47. Ibid., 2:369–70.

48. Ibid., 1:123.

49. *Entretiens*, *Oeuvres*, 12:67; Schrecker, "Parallélisme," p. 241.

50. *Recherche*, *Oeuvres*, 1:453.

51. *Traité de morale*, *Oeuvres*, 11:21.

52. *Méditations chrétiennes*, *Oeuvres*, 10:38.

53. *Philosophe chrétien*, *Oeuvres*, 15:25.

54. *Méditations chrétiennes*, *Oeuvres*, 10:38.

55. Connell, *Vision in God*, pp. 310–13; *Éclaircissements*, 10, *Oeuvres*, 3:137–38.

56. *Traité de morale*, *Oeuvres*, 11:21–22.

57. *Entretiens*, *Oeuvres*, 12:191.

58. *Traité de nature*, *Oeuvres*, 5:27.

59. Bracken, "Problems of Substance," p. 132.

Chapter 6

1. *Éclaircissements*, 10, *Oeuvres*, 3:143.

2. *Entretiens*, *Oeuvres*, 12:174.

3. *Recherche*, *Oeuvres*, 1:457; Gueroult, "Connaissance de Dieu," p. 269.

4. *Recherche*, *Oeuvres*, 2:371.

5. Above, page 74. This shift is seen clearly in the change of expression from the first to the last edition of the *Recherche*. In the edition of 1674 Malebranche wrote that the finite mind cannot know perfectly "the infinite beings"; in the 1712 edition this passage reads simply "the infinite." *Recherche, Oeuvres*, 1:390.

6. Robinet, "Philosophie malebranchiste," p. 227, n. 6.

7. *Entretiens, Oeuvres*, 12:43–44 (italics added).

8. Gueroult, "Preuve malebranchiste," p. 30.

9. *Recherche, Oeuvres*, 2:94–95.

10. *Conversations chrétiennes, Oeuvres*, 4:46.

11. *Prémotion physique, Oeuvres*, 16:117.

12. *Entretiens, Oeuvres*, 12:54.

13. *Philosophe chrétien, Oeuvres*, 15:10.

14. *Méditations chrétiennes, Oeuvres*, 10:40.

15. *Traité de nature, Oeuvres*, 5:26.

16. *Entretiens, Oeuvres*, 12:52–53.

17. *Réponse au livre, Oeuvres*, 6:118; ibid.

18. *Entretiens, Oeuvres*, 12:54.

19. *Recherche, Oeuvres*, 2:100–101 (italics added).

20. Above, page 39.

21. *Recherche, Oeuvres*, 2:93–95.

22. *Recueil, Oeuvres*, 6:245.

23. Anselm, *Proslogium*, pp. 9–10.

24. Gilson, *Spirit of Medieval Philosophy*, p. 60.

25. Leff, *Medieval Thought*, passim; Knowles, *Evolution of Medieval Thought*, passim.

26. Mascall, *He Who Is*, p. 61.

27. *Recherche, Oeuvres*, 2:95.

28. See Copleston, *History of Philosophy*, v. 2, pt. 1:282, for St. Bonaventure's development of this argument.

29. *Prémotion physique, Oeuvres*, 16:132.

30. Aquinas, *Summa Theologiae*, 1:207–9; Mascall, *He Who Is*, pp. 9–10.

31. Cited in Mascall, *He Who Is*, p. 10.

32. Connell, *Vision in God*, p. 219; *Recherche, Oeuvres*, 1:456.

33. Gilson, *Spirit of Medieval Philosophy*, p. 61 (italics added); *Recherche, Oeuvres*, 1:441.

34. *Recherche, Oeuvres*, 2:316; *Éclaircissements*, 15, *Oeuvres*, 3:209–10.

35. *Éclaircissements*, 6, *Oeuvres*, 3:64; Dolson, "Idealism of Malebranche," pp. 398, 403.

36. *Éclaircissements*, 10, *Oeuvres*, 3:131–33, 141; Crocker, *Age of Crisis*, pp. 136–60. Crocker provides a succinct description of the concept of freedom of indifference.

37. *Traité de nature*, *Oeuvres*, 5:28, 46; Randall, *Career of Philosophy*, p. 430.

38. Crocker, *Age of Crisis*, p. 136. "Freedom of indifference was held to signify *action* without motive. On that ground it was rejected not only by the determinists, but also by many of the supporters of freedom, as a form of insanity."

39. *Recherche*, *Oeuvres*, 2:316.

40. *Traité de nature*, *Oeuvres*, 5:66.

41. *Recherche*, *Oeuvres*, 2:313–14.

42. Ibid., 2:316.

43. *Entretiens*, *Oeuvres*, 12:96. See also: *Recherche*, *Oeuvres*, 2:312–13, 316–18; *Éclaircissements*, 15, *Oeuvres*, 3:225–26; *Méditations chrétiennes*, *Oeuvres*, 10:60–61.

44. *Traité de nature*, *Oeuvres*, 5:30.

45. *Recherche*, *Oeuvres*, 1:45.

46. *Entretiens*, *Oeuvres*, 12:96.

47. Randall, *Career of Philosophy*, p. 431.

48. *Recherche*, *Oeuvres*, 2:413ff.

49. Hankins, "Influence of Malebranche," pp. 193–210; Hoskyn, "Malebranche and Leibniz," p. 132.

50. Church, *Philosophy of Malebranche*, pp. 105–6; Siwek, "Optimism in Philosophy," p. 428.

51. Church, "Malebranche and Hume," pp. 143–61; *Philosophy of Malebranche*, pp. 100–101.

52. *Méditations chrétiennes*, *Oeuvres*, 10:96–97.

53. Mascall, *He Who Is*, p. 191.

Chapter 7

1. *Oeuvres*, 1:179.

2. *Recherche*, *Oeuvres*, 2:22; *Pièces jointes*, *Oeuvres*, 17:520.

3. Gouhier, "Philosophie chrétienne," p. 160: see also Hazard, *European Mind*, pt. 2, chapter 4, for "Bossuet at Bay," further evidence of the "anxious soul."

4. Above, pages 87–88; *Recherche*, *Oeuvres*, 2:101.

5. *Éclaircissements*, 10, *Oeuvres*, 3:130.

6. Schrecker, "Parallélisme," p. 244.

7. *Philosophe chrétien*, *Oeuvres*, 15:5.

8. *Recherche*, *Oeuvres*, 2:285.

9. *Pièces jointes*, *Oeuvres*, 17:425–28.

10. *Entretiens*, *Oeuvres*, 12:344.

11. *Traité de nature*, *Oeuvres*, 5:11.

12. *Philosophe chrétien*, *Oeuvres*, 15:7.

13. Again, this formulation marked a departure from the traditional hierarchy of 'substance' that had posited a continuous chain of being from the lowest level of existence (pure potency) to the highest perfection (pure actuality), a continuum characterized by its plenitude. Though abandoning the pattern of 'substance', Malebranche nonetheless retained the assumptions of 'substance'—the intuitive affirmation of being; the plenitude of all being; infinity of perfection in all its positive qualities—in his disjunctive treatment of metaphysics.

14. *Philosophe chrétien*, *Oeuvres*, 15:44.

15. *Recherche*, *Oeuvres*, 2:371–72.

16. Ibid., 1:458.

17. Ibid., 2:374 (italics added).

18. *Éclaircissements*, 10, *Oeuvres*, 3:136.

19. Above, pages 72–73.

20. *Recherche*, *Oeuvres*, 1:61–63.

21. Ibid., 2:291.

22. Ibid., 1:461 (italics added).

23. Ibid., 1:458; 2:365.

24. *Éclaircissements*, 11, *Oeuvres*, 3:167.

25. *Philosophe chrétien*, *Oeuvres*, 15:32.

26. Schrecker, "Parallélisme," p. 233; *Recueil*, *Oeuvres*, 6:201.

27. *Traité de morale*, *Oeuvres*, 11:201.

28. Brunschvicg, *Raison et religion*, p. 140.

29. Iorio, "Intelligible Extension," pp. 180–82.

30. *Entretiens*, *Oeuvres*, 12:42.

31. Copi, *Introduction to Logic*, pp. 308–14. A standard manner of symbolizing universal statements in propositional form is $(x)[Sx \supset Px]$. Rhetorically this reads, 'given any x in the universe, if x is a function of S, the subject of the proposition, then in precisely the same fashion x is a function of P, the predicate of the proposition'.

32. These laws are in evidence in a logic of terms, but as a reflection of being not of thought per se.

33. *Entretiens*, *Oeuvres*, 12:98.

34. On one reading, this is the outcome of Lorenzo Valla's discussion of free will. Although he broke with the rationalistic medieval tradition that had reconciled human free will and divine providence by arguing that all attempts to join the two were irrational, he nonetheless did not infer a denial of God but the limits of the knowing mind. Valla, "On Free Will to Garsia, Bishop of Lerida," trans. and intro. Charles Edward Trinkhaus, Jr., in Cassirer, *Renaissance Philosophy*, pp. 147–82. Trinkhaus's introduction is especially useful.

35. Crocker, *Age of Crisis*, chapter 2.

36. *Recherche*, *Oeuvres*, 1:25.

37. *Entretiens*, *Oeuvres*, 12:101.

38. *Traité de morale*, *Oeuvres*, 11:33–34.

39. Decourtray, "Foi et raison," pp. 67, 86.

40. Gouhier, "Philosophie chrétienne," p. 170; Brunschvicg, *Descartes*, pp. 70, 73.

41. *Oeuvres*, 19:888.

42. *Recherche*, *Oeuvres*, 1:62; also 1:283, 293–99; 2:33–35; *Entretiens*, *Oeuvres*, 12:76.

43. *Traité de morale*, *Oeuvres*, 11:198; *Pièces jointes*, *Oeuvres*, 17:548.

44. *Entretiens*, *Oeuvres*, 12:207.

45. *Traité de morale*, *Oeuvres*, 11:65.

46. *Recherche*, *Oeuvres*, 1:357–58.

47. Boutroux, "L'intellectualisme," p. 27.

48. *Recherche*, *Oeuvres*, 1:17–18.

49. *Éclaircissements*, 17, *Oeuvres*, 3:307.

50. *Entretiens*, *Oeuvres*, 12:95.

51. Ibid., 12:207.

52. *Recherche*, *Oeuvres*, 2:174.

53. Ibid., 1:60–61.

54. Ibid., 2:168.

55. Gueroult, "Connaissance de Dieu," p. 270.

56. *Entretiens*, *Oeuvres*, 12:186.

57. Gueroult, "Connaissance de Dieu," p. 268; *Recherche*, *Oeuvres*, 1:456.

58. *Philosophe chrétien*, *Oeuvres*, 15:48.

59. Ibid., editor's note #17; Aquinas, *Summa Theologiae*, 2:54.

60. *Recherche*, *Oeuvres*, 1:76.

61. Ibid., 1:319.

62. *Entretiens*, *Oeuvres*, 12:133.

63. *Recherche*, *Oeuvres*, 1:319.

64. Schrecker, "Parallélisme," pp. 224–25.

65. *Recherche*, *Oeuvres*, 2:372.

66. Ibid., 2:52.

67. Ibid., 1:66 (italics added).

68. *Entretiens*, *Oeuvres*, 12:30. Here Malebranche describes "truths of faith" as the "principles of our knowledge."

69. Ortega y Gasset, *Idea of Principle*, p. 196.

70. *Recherche*, *Oeuvres*, 2:374.

71. Hazard, *European Mind*, pp. 137–38.

Bibliography

Works of Malebranche

With the completion of the *Oeuvres complètes de Malebranche*, under the general editorship of André Robinet, scholars finally have ready access to all of Malebranche's writings. The enormous task of collating different editions of Malebranche's works, many of them pirated, has been achieved with admirable success and presented in a format that enables the scholar to detect changes in his thought through successive revisions and editions. This is particularly valuable for the *Recherche de la vérité*. In addition to all of Malebranche's published works, the *Oeuvres* contain all notations, short articles, unpublished polemics, and correspondence from the Oratorian's hand, plus extensive selections from his contemporaries in whose works he figures prominently. Finally, the editors have provided extensive indexing and crossreferencing throughout the *Oeuvres*, numerous and invaluable references to contemporary works, thorough biographical material gleaned from contemporary sources, and a complete bibliography of all scholarly works pertaining to Malebranche through 1967. The *Oeuvres*, in short, contain all primary materials pertaining directly to Malebranche, and they deserve to be ranked among the finest critical editions of any author available. A complete listing of the volumes follows.

Bibliography

Malebranche, Nicolas. *Oeuvres complètes*. 20 tomes et index. Direction, André Robinet. "Bibliothèque des textes philosophiques," directeur, Henri Gouhier. Paris: Librairie J. Vrin, 1958–70.

TOMES

I, II, III. *De la Recherche de la vérité: Où l'on traite de la nature de l'esprit de l'homme et de l'usage qu'il en doit faire pour éviter l'erreur dans les sciences*. Édité par Geneviève Rodis-Lewis, Avant-propos de Henri Gouhier.

    I. *Livres I–III*. 1962.

    II. *Livres IV–VI*. 1963.

    III. *Éclaircissements*, 1964.

    IV. *Conversations chrétiennes, dans lesquelles on justifie la vérité de la religion et de la morale de Jésus-Christ*. Publié par André Robinet. 1959.

    V. *Traité de la nature et de la grâce*. Édité par Ginette Dreyfus. 1958.

VI–VII
and
VIII–IX. *Recueil de toutes les réponses a Monsieur Arnauld*. Édité par André Robinet. 1966. (Tomes VI–VII and VIII–IX are each combined in a single volume.)

    VI–VII. *Réponse au livre des vraies et des fausses idées. Trois lettres touchant la défense de M. Arnauld. Quatre lettres touchant celles de M. Arnauld. Dissertation sur les miracles*.

    VIII–IX. *Réponse au livre I des réflexions philosophiques. Deux lettres touchant les. II. et III. vol. des réflexions. Réponse a la troisième lettre de M. Arnauld. Réponse aux lettres I et II de M. Arnauld. Lettres I, II, III d'Arnauld. Écrit contre la prévention et abrégé du Traité de la nature et de la grâce*.

    X. *Méditations chrétiennes et métaphysiques*. Édité par Henri Gouhier et André Robinet. 1967.

    XI. *Traité de morale*. Édité par Michel Adam. 1966.

XII–XIII. *Entretiens sur la métaphysique et sur la religion. Entretiens sur la mort*. Édité par André Robinet. 1965. (Tomes XII–XIII are combined in a single volume.)

Bibliography

XIV. *Traité de l'amour de Dieu. Trois lettres et réponse générale au R. P. Lamy.* Édité par André Robinet. 1963.

XV. *Entretien d'un philosophe chrétien et d'un philosophe chinois sur l'existence et la nature de Dieu.* Édité par André Robinet. 1958.

XVI. *Réflexions sur la prémotion physique.* Publié par André Robinet. 1958.

XVII–1. *Pièces jointes. Écrits divers.* Includes: *Des lois du movement. Polémique avec Regis. Les petites méditations. Polémique avec le Valois.* Publiés par Pierre Costabel, Armand Cuvillier, et André Robinet. 1960.

XVII–2. *Mathematica.* Édité par Pierre Costabel. 1967.

XVIII. *Correspondance, actes, et documents: 1638–1689.* Recueillis et présentés par André Robinet. 1961.

XIX. *Correspondance, actes, et documents: 1690–1715.* Recueillis et présentés par André Robinet. 1961.

XX. *Malebranche vivant: Documents biographiques et bibliographiques.* Recueillis et presentés par André Robinet. 1967.

Index. *Index des citations bibliques. Index des citations patristiques. Index des citations philosophiques et scientifiques.* Par Pierre Clair, Michel Lacombe, et André Robinet. 1970.

Other Primary Sources

André, Y. M. *La vie du R. P. Malebranche.* Paris: P. Ingold, 1886; reprint ed., Geneva, Slatkine Reprints, 1970.

Anselm (St.). *Proslogium; Monologium; An Appendix in Behalf of the Fool by Gaunilon; and Cur Deus Homo.* Trans. Sidney Norton Deane. La Salle, Ill.: The Open Court Publishing Company, 1958 [© 1903].

Aquinas, Thomas. *Summa Theologiae: Part One, Questions 1–26.* 2 vols. Trans. and ed. under direction of Thomas Gilby, O. P. Garden City, N.Y.: Image Books, 1969.

Aristotle. *Metaphysics.* Vol. IV of *The Student's Oxford Aristotle.* Trans. under direction of W. D. Ross. New York: Oxford University Press, 1942.

Arnauld, Antoine. *Oeuvres philosophiques.* Nouv. ed. par Jules Simon. Paris: A. Delahays, 1843.

Augustine (St.). *On Free Choice of the Will.* Trans. Anna S. Benjamin

Bibliography

and L. H. Hackstaff. New York: The Bobbs-Merrill Company, Inc., 1964.

Cassirer, Ernst; Kristeller, Paul Oskar; and Randall, John Herman, Jr., eds. *The Renaissance Philosophy of Man*. Chicago: University of Chicago Press, 1948.

de Cordemoy, Geraud. *Le discernement du corps et de l'âme*. Paris: n.p., 1679.

Descartes, René. *Oeuvres*. 12 tomes. Publiés par Charles Adam et Paul Tannery, sous les auspices du Ministère de l'Instruction Publique. Paris: Librairie Philosophique J. Vrin, 1896–1910.

_____. *Oeuvres philosophiques*. 3 tomes. Ed. Ferdinand Alquié. Paris: Éditions Garnier Frères, 1963.

_____. *Philosophical Letters*. Trans. and ed. Anthony Kenny. Oxford: Clarendon Press, 1970.

_____. *The Philosophical Works of Descartes*. 2 vols. Trans. Elizabeth S. Haldane and G. R. T. Ross. Cambridge: University Press, c. 1911, reprint with corrections, 1970.

Fontenelle, Bernard le Bovier de. *Pages choisies de grands écrivains: Fontenelle*. Ed. and intro. Henri Potez. Paris: Librairie Armand Colin, 1909.

Foucher, Simon. *Critique de la Recherche de la vérité*. Ed. with intro. Richard A. Watson. New York and London: Johnson Reprint Corporation, 1969. (Facsimile reprint of the 1675 edition.)

Leibniz, Gottfried Wilhelm. *Philosophical Papers and Letters*. 2nd ed. Sel., trans., ed., and intro. Leroy E. Loemker. Dordrecht, Holland: D. Reidel Publishing Company, 1969.

Locke, John. "An Examination of P. Malebranche's Opinion of Seeing All Things in God," in *The Works of John Locke: A New Edition, Corrected*. Vol. IX. London, 1823. (Reprinted by Scientia Verlag Allen, Germany, 1963.)

McKeon, Richard, ed. and trans. *Selections from Medieval Philosophers*. 2 vols. New York: Charles Scribner's Sons, 1929.

Pascal, Blaise. *Oeuvres complètes*. Présentation et notes de Louis Lafuma. Paris: Éditions du Seuil—The Macmillan Company, 1963.

Robinet, André, ed. *Malebranche et Leibniz; relations personelles, présentées avec les textes complets des auteurs et de leurs correspondants revus, corrigés et inédits*. Paris: Librairie Philosophique J. Vrin, 1955.

Bibliography

Secondary Sources

BOOKS

Balz, Albert G. A. *Cartesian Studies*. New York: Columbia University Press, 1951.

———. *Descartes and the Modern Mind*. New Haven and London: Yale University Press and Oxford University Press, 1952.

Barber, W. H. *Leibniz in France: From Arnauld to Voltaire; A Study in French Reactions to Leibnizianism, 1670–1760*. Oxford: Clarendon Press, 1955.

Barbour, Ian G. *Issues in Science and Religion*. New York: Harper & Row, Publishers, 1971 [© 1966].

———. *Myths, Models and Paradigms: A Comparative Study in Science and Religion*. New York: Harper & Row, Publishers, 1974.

Beck, Leslie John. *The Metaphysics of Descartes*. London: Oxford University Press, 1965.

———. *The Method of Descartes*. London: Oxford University Press, 1952.

Belaval, Yvon. *Leibniz critique de Descartes*. Paris: Librairie Gallimard, 1960.

Bell, Eric Temple. *Mathematics: Queen and Servant of Science*. New York: McGraw-Hill, 1951.

Beth, Evert W. *Mathematical Thought: An Introduction to the Philosophy of Mathematics*. Dordrecht, Holland: D. Reidel Publishing Company, 1965.

Black, Max. *Models and Metaphors: Studies in Language and Philosophy*. Ithaca, N.Y.: Cornell University Press, 1962.

———. *The Nature of Mathematics*. New York: The Humanities Press, 1950.

Blanchard, Pierre. *L'attention à Dieu selon Malebranche*. Paris: Desclée de Brouwer, 1956.

Boas, Marie. *The Scientific Renaissance: 1450–1630*. New York: Harper & Row, Publishers, 1962.

Bochner, Salomon. *The Role of Mathematics in the Rise of Science*. Princeton, N.J.: Princeton University Press, 1966.

Bouiller, Francisque. *Histoire de la philosophie cartésienne*. 2 tomes, 3e ed. Paris: Durand, 1868.

Boyer, Carl B. *A History of Mathematics*. New York: John Wiley and Sons, 1968.

Bibliography

Bridet, L. *La theorie de la connaissance dans la philosophie de Malebranche.* Paris: M. Rivière, 1929.

Brown, Colin. *Philosophy and the Christian Faith: A Historical Sketch from the Middle Ages to the Present Day.* London: The Tyndale Press, 1968.

Brunschvicg, Léon. *Écrits philosophiques: Tome premier; L'humanisme de l'occident; Descartes–Spinoza–Kant.* Paris: Presses Universitaires de France, 1951.

———. *Les étapes de la philosophie mathématique.* Paris: Presses Universitaires de France, 1947.

———. *Le progrès de la conscience dans la philosophie occidentale.* Tome premier. Paris: Librairie Félix Alcan, 1927.

———. *La raison et la religion.* Paris: Librairie Félix Alcan, 1939.

———. *René Descartes.* Paris: Les Éditions Rieder, 1937.

———. *Spinoza et ses contemporains.* 4ᵉ ed. Paris: Presses Universitaires de France, 1951.

Burtt, Edwin Arthur. *The Metaphysical Foundations of Modern Physical Science.* Garden City, N.Y.: Doubleday & Company, Inc., 1954 [© 1924].

Butler, R. J., ed. *Cartesian Studies.* New York: Barnes and Noble, 1972.

Butterfield, Herbert. *The Origins of Modern Science: 1300–1800.* Rev. ed. New York: The Free Press, 1965 [© 1957].

Calvet, Jean. *La littérature religieuse de François de Sales à Fénelon.* Tome V en *Histoire de la littérature française.* Ed. J. Calvet. Paris: Éditions Mondiales, 1956.

Cassirer, Ernst. *The Individual and the Cosmos in Renaissance Philosophy.* Trans. Mario Domandi. Philadelphia: University of Pennsylvania Press, 1972.

———. *The Platonic Renaissance in England.* Trans. James P. Pettegrove. Austin: University of Texas Press, 1953.

———. *Substance and Function* and *Einstein's Theory of Relativity.* Trans. W. C. Swabey and M. C. Swabey. New York: Dover Publications, Inc., 1953.

Centre international de synthèse. *Malebranche: L'homme et l'oeuvre; 1638–1715.* "Journées Malebranche, organisées au Centre international de synthèse; salon de Madame de Lambert, les 5, 6, 7 Juin 1965." Paris: Librairie Philosophique J. Vrin, 1967.

Church, Ralph Withington. *A Study in the Philosophy of Malebranche.* London: George Allen & Unwin, Ltd., 1931.

Bibliography

Collingwood, R. G. *The Idea of Nature*. New York: Oxford University Press, 1960 [© 1945].

———. *Speculum Mentis: Or the Map of Knowledge*. London: Oxford University Press, 1924.

Connell, Desmond. *The Vision in God: Malebranche's Scholastic Sources*. Louvain: Editions Nauwelaerts; Paris: Beatrice Nauwelaerts, 1967.

Copi, Irving M. *Introduction to Logic*. 2nd ed. New York: The Macmillan Company, 1961.

Copleston, Frederick, S.J. *A History of Philosophy*. Vols. 1 and 2. Garden City, N.Y.: Doubleday & Company, Inc., 1962 [© 1946, 1950].

Cragg, G. R. *The Church and the Age of Reason: 1648–1789*. Vol. IV in *The Pelican History of the Church*. Ed. Owen Chadwick. Middlesex, Eng.: Penguin Books, 1960.

Crocker, Lester G. *An Age of Crisis: Man and World in Eighteenth Century French Thought*. Baltimore: Johns Hopkins Press, 1959.

Cuvillier, Armand. *Essai sur la mystique de Malebranche*. Paris: J. Vrin, 1954.

Dantzig, Tobias. *Aspects of Science*. New York: The Macmillan Company, 1937.

———. *Number: The Language of Science*. 4th ed., rev. and enl. Garden City, N.Y.: Doubleday & Co., 1954.

Delbos, Victor. *Étude de la philosophie de Malebranche*. Paris: Bloud & Gay, 1924.

———. *La philosophie française*. Paris: Librairie Plon, 1919.

Dijksterhuis, E. J. *The Mechanization of the World Picture*. Trans. C. Dikshoorn. London: Oxford University Press, 1961.

Doney, Willis, ed. *Descartes: A Collection of Critical Essays*. Garden City, N.Y.: Doubleday & Co., 1967.

Dreyfus, Ginette. *La volonté selon Malebranche*. Paris: J. Vrin, 1958.

Dupuy, Michel. *Berulle et le sacerdoce: Étude historique et doctrinal*. "Textes Inedits." Paris: Bibliothèque d'histoire et d'archéologie chrétiennes, 1969.

Enriques, Federigo. *The Historic Development of Logic: The Principles and Structure of Science in the Conception of Mathematical Thinkers*. Trans. Jerome Rosenthal. New York: Russell and Russell, 1968.

Ferré, Frederick. *Language, Logic, and God*. New York: Harper & Row, Publishers, 1969.

Gibson, A. Boyce. *The Philosophy of Descartes*. New York: Russell & Russell, 1932.

Bibliography

Gilson, Étienne. *Études sur le role de la pensée médiévale dans la formation du système cartésien*. Paris, 1938.

————. *God and Philosophy*. New Haven: Yale University Press, 1941.

————. *La liberté chez Descartes et la théologie*. Paris: F. Alcan, 1913.

————. *The Spirit of Medieval Philosophy*. Trans. A. H. C. Downes. New York: Charles Scribner's Sons, 1936.

————. *The Unity of Philosophical Experience*. New York: Charles Scribner's Sons, 1937.

Gouhier, Henri. *Essais sur Descartes*. Paris: Librairie Philosophique J. Vrin, 1937.

————. *La philosophie de Malebranche et son expérience religieuse*. Paris: Librairie Philosophique J. Vrin, 1926.

————. *La vocation de Malebranche*. Paris: Librairie Philosophique J. Vrin, 1926.

Gueroult, Martial. *Malebranche*. 3 tomes. Paris: Aubier, 1955, 1959.

Haldane, E. S. *Descartes, His Life and Times*. London: Murray, 1905.

Hazard, Paul. *The European Mind: 1680–1715*. Trans. J. Lewis May. New York: The World Publishing Company, 1963.

Keeling, S. V. *Descartes*. 2nd ed. London: Oxford University Press, 1968.

Kenny, Anthony. *Descartes: A Study of His Philosophy*. New York: Random House, 1968.

Kline, Morris. *Mathematics and the Physical World*. New York: Thomas Y. Crowell Company, 1959.

Knowles, David. *The Evolution of Medieval Thought*. New York: Random House, 1962.

Koyré, Alexandre. *From the Closed World to the Infinite Universe*. Baltimore and London: The Johns Hopkins Press, 1957.

Kristeller, Paul Oskar. *Renaissance Thought: The Classic, Scholastic and Humanist Strains*. A rev. and enl. ed. of *The Classics and Renaissance Thought*. New York: Harper & Row, Publishers, 1961.

Kuhn, Thomas S. *The Structure of Scientific Revolutions*. 2nd ed., enl. Vol. 2, no. 2, of *International Encyclopedia of Unified Science*. Chicago: University of Chicago Press, 1970.

Labbas, Lucien. *L'idée de science dans Malebranche et son originalité*. Paris: J. Vrin, 1931.

Laporte, Jean. *Études d'histoire de la philosophie française au XVIIᵉ siècle*. Paris: Librairie Philosophique J. Vrin, 1951.

Leff, Gordon. *Medieval Thought: St. Augustine to Ockham*. Baltimore: Penguin Books, 1958.

Bibliography

Lévy-Bruhl, Lucien. *History of Modern Philosophy in France*. Reprint ed. Chicago and London: The Open Court Publishing Company, 1924.

Leyden, W. von. *Seventeenth Century Metaphysics: An Examination of some Main Concepts and Theories*. London: Gerald Duckworth & Co., Ltd., 1968.

Loemker, Leroy E. *Struggle for Synthesis: The Seventeenth Century Background of Leibniz's Synthesis of Order and Freedom*. Cambridge, Mass.: Harvard University Press, 1972.

Lovejoy, Arthur O. *The Great Chain of Being: A Study in the History of an Idea*. New York: Harper & Row, Publishers, 1960 [© 1936].

Luce, A. A. *Berkeley and Malebranche: A Study in the Origins of Berkeley's Thought*. London: Oxford University Press, 1934.

Lukasiewicz, Jan. *Aristotle's Syllogistic: From the Standpoint of Modern Formal Logic*. 2nd ed. London: Oxford University Press, 1957.

Maritain, J. *The Dream of Descartes*. Trans. Maybelle L. Audison. London: Editions Poetry, 1946.

Mascall, E. L. *He Who Is: A Study in Traditional Theism*. London: Longmans, Green and Co., 1943.

———. *Words and Images: A Study in Theological Discourse*. London: Longmans, Green and Co., 1957.

Meyer, R. W. *Leibniz and the 17th Century Revolution*. Trans. J. P. Stern. Cambridge: Bowes and Bowes, 1952.

Mouy, Paul. *Le développement de la physique cartésienne, 1646–1712*. Paris: J. Vrin, 1934.

———. *Les lois du choc des corps d'après Malebranche*. Paris: Librairie Philosophique J. Vrin, 1927.

Ortega y Gasset, José. *The Idea of Principle in Leibniz and the Evolution of Deductive Theory*. Trans. Mildred Adams. New York: W. W. Norton & Co., Inc., 1971.

Perraud, P. Adolphe. *L'oratoire de France: Au XVIIe et au XIXe siècle*. Deuxième édition. Paris: Charles Douniol, Librairie-éditeur, 1866.

Poincaré, Henri. *The Foundations of Science*. Trans. George Bruce Halstead. *Science and Education Series*, ed. J. M. Cattell. Includes *Science and Hypothesis*; *The Value of Science*; *Science and Method*. New York: Science Press, 1929.

———. *Mathematics and Science: Last Essays*. Trans. John W. Bolduc. New York: Dover Publications, Inc., 1963 [© 1913].

Popkin, Richard H. *The History of Scepticism from Erasmus to Descartes*. Rev. ed. New York: Harper & Row, Publishers, 1964.

Bibliography

Radner, Daisie. *Malebranche: A Study of a Cartesian System*. Amsterdam: Van Gorcum & Comp., 1978.

Randall, John Herman, Jr. *Aristotle*. New York: Columbia University Press, 1960.

_____. *The Career of Philosophy: From the Middle Ages to Enlightenment*. New York and London: Columbia University Press, 1962.

Robinet, André. *Système et existence dans l'oeuvre de Malebranche*. Paris: Librairie Philosophique J. Vrin, 1965.

Rome, Beatrice K. *The Philosophy of Malebranche: A Study of His Integration of Faith, Reason, and Experimental Observation*. Chicago: Henry Regnery Company, 1963.

Russell, Bertrand. *Introduction to Mathematical Philosophy*. New York: The Macmillan Company, 1919.

Saisset, Émile. *Precurseurs et disciples de Descartes*. Genève: Slatkine Reprints, 1969 [Réimpression de l'édition de Paris, 1862].

Scholz, Heinrich. *Concise History of Logic*. Trans. Kurt F. Leidecker. New York: Philosophical Library, 1961.

Smith, Norman. *New Studies in the Philosophy of Descartes*. London: Macmillan, 1952.

Strong, Edward W. *Procedures and Metaphysics: A Study in the Philosophy of Mathematical-Physical Science in the Sixteenth and Seventeenth Centuries*. Berkeley, Calif.: University of California Press, 1936.

Struik, Dirk J. *A Concise History of Mathematics*. 2nd ed. New York: Dover Publications, Inc., 1948.

Vrooman, Jack Rochford. *René Descartes: A Biography*. New York: G. P. Putnam's Sons, 1970.

Vuillemin, Jules. *Mathématiques et métaphysique chez Descartes*. Paris: Presses Universitaires de France, 1960.

Waismann, Friedrich. *Introduction to Mathematical Thinking*. Trans. Thedore J. Benac. New York: Harper & Row, Publishers, 1959.

Watson, Richard A. *The Downfall of Cartesianism: 1673–1712*. The Hague: Martinus Nijhoff, 1966.

White, Hayden. *Metahistory: The Historical Imagination in Nineteenth-Century Europe*. Baltimore & London: The Johns Hopkins University Press, 1973.

Whitehead, Alfred North. *An Introduction to Mathematics*. New York: Oxford University Press, 1958 [© 1911].

_____. *Science and the Modern World*. New York: The Macmillan Company, 1925. (Reissued by The New American Library, Mentor Books, 1948.)

Bibliography

_____. *Science and Philosophy*. Paterson, N.J.: Littlefield, Adams, & Co., 1964 [© 1948].

Willey, Basil. *The Seventeenth Century Background: Studies in the Thought of the Age in Relation to Poetry and Religion*. Garden City, N.Y.: Doubleday & Company, Inc., 1953 [© 1934].

ARTICLES

Balz, Albert G. A. "Cartesian Refutations of Spinoza." *The Philosophical Review* 46, no. 5 (1937): 461–84.

Bergmann, Gustav. "Some Remarks on the Philosophy of Malebranche." *The Review of Metaphysics* 10, no. 2 (1956): 207–26.

Blondel, Charles. "La psychologie de Malebranche." *Revue internationale de philosophie* 1, no. 1 (1938): 59–76.

Blondel, Maurice. "L'anti-cartésianisme de Malebranche." *Revue de métaphysique et de morale* 23 (1916): 1–25.

Boutroux, Émile. "L'intellectualisme de Malebranche." *Revue de métaphysique et de morale* 23 (1916): 26–36.

Bracken, Harry M. "Berkeley and Malebranche on Ideas." *The Modern Schoolman* 41 (1963): 1–15.

_____. "Some Problems of Substance among the Cartesians." *American Philosophical Quarterly* 1, no. 2 (1964): 129–37.

Bréhier, Émile. "Les 'jugements naturels' chez Malebranche." *Revue philosophique de la France et de l'étranger* 125 (1938): 142–50.

Bruch, Jean-Louis. "La combinatoire de Malebranche." *Revue de métaphysique et de morale* 68, no. 3 (1963): 319–33.

Brunschvicg, Léon. "Mathématique et métaphysique chez Descartes." *Revue de métaphysique et de morale* 34, no. 3 (1927): 277–324.

Campbell, Hilbert H. "Addison's 'Cartesian' Passage and Nicolas Malebranche." *Philological Quarterly* 46, no. 3 (1967): 408–12.

Cassirer, Ernst. "La place de la 'Recherche de la vérité par la lumière naturelle' dans l'oeuvre de Descartes." *Revue philosophique de la France et de l'étranger* 127 (1939): 261–300.

_____. "Some Remarks on the Question of the Originality of the Renaissance." *Journal of the History of Ideas* 4, no. 1 (1943): 49–56.

Church, Ralph Withington. "Malebranche and Hume." *Revue internationale de philosophie* 1, no. 1 (1938): 143–61.

Connell, Desmond. "Gassendi and the Genesis of Malebranche's

Bibliography

Philosophy." *Actes du XIIème congrès international de philosophie* 13.
Venice: Firenze Sansoni Editore (1961): 109–13.

———. "La passivité de l'entendement selon Malebranche." *Revue philosophique de Louvain* 53 (1955): 542–65.

Davies, Arthur Ernest. "Some Factors of Malebranche's Theory of Knowledge." *The Philosophical Review* 33, no. 5 (1924): 479–97.

Decourtray, Albert. "Foi et raison chez Malebranche." *Mélanges de science religieuse* 10, no. 1 (1953): 67–86.

De Lattre, Alain. "La ferveur malebranchiste et l'ordre des raisons." *Revue philosophique de la France et de l'étranger* 151, no. 1 (1961): 73–86 (Part One); 152, no. 3 (1962): 359–64 (Part Two); 154, no. 1 (1964): 90–102 (Part Three).

———. "La volonté chez Malebranche et les contradictions de la doctrine." *Revue philosophique de la France et de l'étranger* 154, no. 1 (1964): 103–9.

Dolson, G. L. "The Idealism of Malebranche." *The Philosophical Review* 15, no. 4 (1906): 387–405.

Doney, Willis. "The Cartesian Circle." *Journal of the History of Ideas* 16, no. 4 (1955): 324–38.

Dorter, Kenneth. "First Philosophy: Metaphysics or Epistemology?" *Dialogue* 11, no. 1 (1972), 1–22.

Doxsee, Carll Whitman. "Hume's Relation to Malebranche." *The Philosophical Review* 25, no. 5 (1916): 692–710.

Dreyfus, Ginette. "Les différents aspects de la liberté humaine chez Malebranche." *Revue de métaphysique et de morale* 51, no. 2 (1946): 142–65 (Part One); 51, no. 3 (1946): 239–58 (Part Two).

Dumas, Jean-Louis. "Les études malebranchistes en France." *Les études philosophiques* 20, no. 3 (1965): 319–28.

Frankfurt, Harry G. "Descartes' Discussion of his Existence in the Second Meditation." *The Philosophical Review* 75, no. 3 (1966): 329–56.

———. "Descartes' Validation of Reason." *American Philosophical Quarterly* 2, no. 2 (1965): 149–56.

———. "Memory and the Cartesian Circle." *The Philosophical Review* 71 (1962): 504–11.

Fritz, Anita Dunlevy. "Berkeley's Self—Its Origin in Malebranche." *Journal of the History of Ideas* 15, no. 4 (1954): 554–72.

———. "Malebranche and the Immaterialism of Berkeley." *Review of Metaphysics* 3, no. 1 (1949): 59–80.

Getchev, George S. "Some of Malebranche's Reactions to Spinoza as

Bibliography

Revealed in His Correspondence with Dourtous de Mairan." *The Philosophical Review* 41, no. 4 (1932): 385–94.

Gewirth, Alan. "Clearness and Distinctness in Descartes." *Philosophy* 18, no. 69 (1943): 17–36.

———. "Experience and the Non-Mathematical in the Cartesian Method." *Journal of the History of Ideas* 2, no. 2 (1941): 183–210.

Girbal, F. "Informations historiques et documents à propos de Malebranche et de Bernard Lamy." *Revue internationale de philosophie* 32, no. 2 (1955): 288–90.

Gouhier, Henri. "Introduction bibliographique à l'oeuvre et à la pensée de Malebranche." *Revue internationale de philosophie* 1, no. 1 (1938): 162–74.

———. "Philosophie chrétienne et théologie: à propos de la seconde polémique de Malebranche." *Revue philosophique de la France et de l'étranger* 125 (1938): 151–93.

Gueroult, Martial. "La connaissance de Dieu chez Malebranche." *De la connaissance de Dieu: Recherches de philosophie*. Tomes 3, 4. Paris: Desclée de Brouwer (1958): 267–306.

———. "Métaphysique et physique de la force chez Descartes et chez Malebranche." *Revue de métaphysique et de morale* 59, nos. 1 & 2 (1954): 1–37; 113–34.

———. "La preuve malebranchiste de 'simple vue'." *Actes du XIᵉᵐᵉ congrès international de philosophie*. Amsterdam: North-Holland Publishing Company (1953): 30–35.

Hankins, Thomas L. "The Influence of Malebranche on the Science of Mechanics During the Eighteenth Century." *Journal of the History of Ideas* 28, no. 2 (1967): 193–210.

Hollinger, David A. "T. S. Kuhn's Theory of Science and Its Implications for History." *The American Historical Review* 78, no. 2 (1973): 370–93.

Hoskyn, Fred Percy. "The Relation of Malebranche and Leibniz on Questions in Cartesian Physics." *The Monist* 40 (1930): 131–45.

Iyengar, K. R. Sreenivasa. "The Nature of Descartes's Method." In *Travaux du IXᵉ congrès international de philosophie: Études cartésiennes*. Actualités scientifiques et industrielles, no. 530, vol. 2. Paris: Hermann et Cⁱᵉ editeurs (1937): 15–20.

Johnston, Charlotte. "Locke's *Examination of Malebranche* and John Norris." *Journal of the History of Ideas* 19, no. 4 (1958): 551–58.

Klopke, John R. "Malebranche Revisited." *The New Scholasticism* 39, no. 2 (1965): 189–208.

Bibliography

Laird, John. "The 'Legend' of Arnauld's Realism." *Mind* 33, no. 130 (1924): 176–79.

_____. "Malebranche." *Philosophy* 2, no. 41 (1936): 32–47.

Laporte, Jean. "L'idée de 'liaison nécessaire' chez Descartes." In *Travaux du IXe congrès international de philosophie: Études cartésiennes.* Actualités scientifiques et industrielles, no. 530, vol. 2. Paris: Hermann et Cie, editeurs (1937): 9–14.

_____. "La liberté selon Malebranche." *Revue de métaphysique et de morale* 45 (1938): 339–410.

Lewis, Geneviève. "L'âme et la durée d'après une controverse cartésienne." *Revue internationale de philosophie* 4, no. 12 (1950): 190–209.

_____. "L'intervention de Nicole dans la polémique entre Arnauld et Malebranche, d'après des lettres inédites." *Revue philosophique de la France et de l'étranger* 140 (1950): 483–507.

Loemker, Leroy E. "A Note on the Origin and Problem of Leibniz's Discourse of 1686." *Journal of the History of Ideas* 8, no. 4 (1947): 449–66.

Lovejoy, Arthur O. "Reply to Professor Laird." *Mind* 33, no. 130 (1924): 180–81.

_____. " 'Representative Ideas' in Malebranche and Arnauld." *Mind* 32, no. 128 (1923): 449–61.

McRae, Robert. " 'Idea' as a Philosophical Term in the Seventeenth Century." *Journal of the History of Ideas* 26, no. 2 (1965): 175–90.

_____. "The Unity of the Sciences: Bacon, Descartes, and Leibniz." *Journal of the History of Ideas* 18, no. 1 (1957): 27–48.

Miller, James. "Descartes' Conceptualism." *The Review of Metaphysics* 4, no. 2 (1950): 239–46.

Moreau, Joseph. "Le réalisme de Malebranche et la fonction de l'idée." *Revue de métaphysique et de morale* 51 (1946): 97–141.

Nagel, Ernest. " 'Impossible Numbers': A Chapter in the History of Modern Logic." *Studies in the History of Ideas.* Vol. 3. Ed., Columbia University Department of Philosophy. New York: Columbia University Press (1935): 429–74.

Robinet, André. "Clés pour Malebranche." *Nouvelles littéraires* 43, no. 1970 (1965): 4.

_____. "Conception tragique et conception optimiste de la nature humaine dans la philosophie de Malebranche." *Les études philosophiques* 16, no. 3 (1961): 317–21.

_____. "Le groupe malebranchiste introducteur du Calcul

Bibliography

infinitésimal en France." *Revue d'histoire des sciences et de leurs applications* 13 (1960): 287–308.

————. "Jean Prestet ou la bonne foi cartésienne (1648–1691)." *Revue d'histoire des sciences et de leurs applications* 13 (1960): 95–104.

————. "Malebranche dans la pensée de Fontenelle." *Revue de synthèse* 82 (1961): 79–86.

————. "Un opuscule inédit de Malebranche—De la prédestination." *Revue de métaphysique et de morale* 62, no. 1 (1957): 1–8.

————. "La philosophie malebranchiste des mathématiques." *Revue d'histoire des sciences et de leurs applications* 14 (1961): 205–54.

————. "La vocation académicienne de Malebranche." *Revue d'histoire des sciences et de leurs applications* 12, no. 1 (1959): 1–18.

Rochot, B. "Malebranche et son temps." *Revue de synthèse* 85, no. 36 (1964): 57–62.

Rodis-Lewis, Geneviève. "Le domaine propre de l'homme chez les Cartésiens." *Journal of the History of Philosophy* 2, no. 2 (1964): 157–88.

Salmon, Elizabeth G. "Mathematical Roots of Cartesian Metaphysics." *The New Scholasticism* 39, no. 2 (1965): 158–69.

Schrecker, Paul. "Arnauld, Malebranche, Prestet, et la theorie de nombres negatifs." *Thales* 2 (1935): 82–90.

————. "Malebranche et les mathématiques." *Travaux du IXe congrès international de philosophie. Études cartésiennes.* Actualités scientifiques et industrielles, no. 530, vol. 2. Paris: Hermann et Cie, editeurs (1937): 33–40.

————. "Malebranche et le préformisme biologique." *Revue internationale de philosophie* 1, no. 1 (1938): 77–97.

————. "Le parallélisme théologico-mathématique chez Malebranche." *Revue philosophique de la France et de l'étranger* 125 (1938): 215–52.

Siwek, Paul. "Optimism in Philosophy." *The New Scholasticism* 22, no. 4 (1948): 417–39.

Smith, Norman. "Malebranche's Theory of the Perception of Distance and Magnitude." *British Journal of Psychology* 1, no. 3 (1905): 191–204.

Thamin, R. "Le traité de morale de Malebranche." *Revue de métaphysique et de morale* 23 (1916): 93–126.

Van Breda, Herman Leo. "Les journées Malebranche." *Revue philosophique de Louvain* 63, no. 80 (1965): 630–44.

Bibliography

DISSERTATION

Iorio, Dominick Anthony. "The Notion of Intelligible Extension in
Nicolas Malebranche." Ph.D. dissertation, Fordham University,
1966.

Index

Index

Index

Index

Index

Index

Malebranche's theory of, 47–48, 60–63; influence on metaphysics, 100–103, 108; and infinity of God, 112–13, 115, 129–33; relations of hypostatized, 127, 134–35, 147; and logic of propositions, 153–54 (n. 10). *See also* Algebra; Arithmetic; Calculus; Geometry; Magnitude(s); 'Number'; *Unité*

Matter, 93, 112, 134–36; Descartes on, 30, 35; and mind, 77, 93–94, 96–97, 107, 110, 112, 120–23; modifications of, 95, 121–22, 126. *See also* Mind, and matter

Measure: common, 52; exact, 60

Mechanics: and geometry, 55

Meditations on First Philosophy, 41

Mersenne, Marin, 28–30, 128

Mesland, Denis, 40

Metaphysics, 5, 12, 34, 100, 144, 168 (n. 13); Aristotle on, 11, 38; related to model of 'substance', 91–109; assumptions of in Malebranche, 110–27; and religion, 128, 143. *See also* Being; God; Reality; 'Substance'

Method, 94. *See also* Descartes, 'number' in; Epistemology; 'Number'; Truth(s)

Mind, 35, 56, 69, 72, 85, 93; modifications of, 72, 96–97, 121–22, 125–26; and matter, 77, 93–94, 96–97, 107, 110, 112, 120–23. *See also* Matter; Substance(s)

Miracles, 45, 143

Model(s), 34, 46, 98, 125, 128, 135; theory of, 5–7; of 'substance', 8–13; of 'number', 8, 13–22. *See also* Archetype(s); 'Number'; 'Substance'

Modification(s): of mind, 72, 96–97, 121–22, 125–26; of matter, 95, 121–22, 126; Malebranche's theory of, 95–102, 104, 108, 164 (n. 19)

Montaigne, Michel Eyquem de, 12, 163 (n. 47)

Motion, 93, 123; laws of, 83, 122–23

Nature: law of, 82

Necessity, 44, 107, 115, 123, 134; ontological, 39, 121–22, 133; in relations, 56–57, 102–3; in God's will, 122, 124–25; mathematical, 127, 132–33

Neoplatonism, 118

Newton, Isaac, 16, 65, 91

Non-being, 10, 101–2, 132. *See also* Being; Nothingness

Noncontradiction, 101, 139

Nothingness, 100–102

Number(s), 4, 58, 60–61, 63, 66, 71, 73, 88; concept of, 13–22, 152 (nn. 35, 36); pure, 14, 20, 33; cardinal concept of, 16–19, 29, 31, 47, 64–65, 68, 72, 81, 85–86, 90; ordinal concept of, 16–19, 47, 64–65, 68, 72, 89; and Descartes, 25–27, 29, 34; intuition of, 54, 76; and magnitude, 59, 88; abstract, 70, 77, 84–86; eternal, 70–71, 78; and infinity, 88, 130

Index

Index

Index